S·E·X

THE MYTH AND THE MAGIC

E. LONNIE MELASHENKO
AND TIMOTHY E. CROSBY

Pacific Press Publishing Association
Boise, Idaho
Oshawa, Ontario, Canada

Edited by Jerry D. Thomas
Cover design by Tim Larson
Cover photo by Don Landwehle/Image Bank ©
Typset in 10/12 New Century Schoolbook

Library of Congress Cataloging-in-Publication Data:

Melashenko, Lonnie, 1947-
    Sex: the myth and the magic / by Lonnie
    Melashenko and Tim Crosby.
        p.   cm.
    ISBN 0-8163-1214-1
    1. Sex—Religious aspects—Christianity.
2. Christian life—1960-
I. Crosby, Timothy, 1954-   . II. Title.
BT708.M44   1993   93-41886
241' .66—dc20   CIP

93 94 95 96 97 • 8 7 6 5 4 3 2 1

Contents

1

Sex Without Sorrow

Do Christian couples have more fun? In bed?

In September 1975 *Redbook* magazine published a survey form which was returned by over 65,000 of its readers. This survey explored the relationship between lifestyle and beliefs. The responses revealed that believers were more satisfied with life and more at peace with themselves than unbelievers. One of the more interesting findings was that those who were more religious scored higher in sexual satisfaction, while the so-called "liberated" women reported a higher degree of sexual dissatisfaction.

This should come as no surprise to Christians. Psalm 16:11 says that in God's right hand are pleasures forevermore. And many Christians have experienced in their own lives the truth of this statement.

Satan also peddles pleasures, of course, but they don't last forever; they don't even last a lifetime. They only last a season and bring sorrow in their train.

In no area of life is the contrast between God's forever pleasures and Satan's vanishing fun more vivid than in the area of sexuality. God invented sex and intended that it should establish a bond between husbands and wives.

A fascinating demonstration of God's approval of sexual pleasure can be found in the little book in the Bible called Song of Solomon. This ancient love poem is filled with sensual imagery. Actually, it is even more sensual than it first appears to modern readers because much of the sexual allusion is couched in figures of speech which are foreign to us. The book is so colorful in its portrayal of sexual enjoyment that ancient rabbinic law forbade anyone under the age of thirty to read it. The rabbis wanted to make sure readers would have the maturity to handle the book's vividness.

Since the Bible is God's Word, it is clear that God does not have a problem with rich sexual enjoyment. And when we follow the biblical guidelines, sexual pleasure has no bitter side effects.

What are the biblical guidelines for sexual relations? Let's examine a passage in the New Testament which gives some rather interesting counsel on marital lovemaking. It is found in 1 Corinthians 7:2-5:

> Since there is so much immorality, each man should have his own wife, and each woman her own husband. The husband should fulfill his marital duty to his wife, and likewise the wife to her husband. The wife's body does not belong to her alone but also to her husband. In the same way, the husband's body does not belong to him alone but also to his wife. Do not deprive each other except by mutual consent and for a time, so that you may devote yourselves to prayer. Then come together again so that Satan will not tempt you because of your lack of self-control.

This passage may come as a bit of a shock for some Christians. Notice that no limits are placed on the sexual expression of love within marriage. On the contrary, limits are placed on abstinence! In plain English, this passage says: If you're married, your body belongs to your spouse as well as to you. You have a duty to give your spouse sexual satisfaction. The only time you may abstain from sexual intercourse is when your spouse agrees to it for purposes of prayer, and even then the period of abstinence should be relatively brief, so that neither of you will be tempted to find satisfaction somewhere else.

The focus of this passage is on responsibility instead of rights. Nothing is said about what your spouse owes you, instead the focus is on what you owe your spouse. Therefore sex must neither be compelled as "my right" nor withheld as a bargaining chip, but rather offered freely as a gift.

This attitude of self-giving is the basis of fulfilling sexual union. If both husband and wife approach their times of sexual intimacy with a determination to give pleasure and happiness to the other, then both will experience increased satisfaction. This is probably the reason faithful Christians often have a more satisfying sex life.

Let me speak specifically to husbands. When your wife is not feeling well, you should not try to force yourself upon her and demand your conjugal rights. Love cannot be coerced. Rather than badgering your wife into submission, woo her. Gently meet her needs and fulfill her desires. For women, tenderness is a turn-on.

Some husbands have a rather selfish approach to sex. They never take the time to give pleasure to their wives, proceeding quickly to a climax without concern for her needs. The most frequent sexual complaint of women is a lack of foreplay. No wonder some wives have no desire for sex!

It is important to respect your wife. Uncleanness, body odor, or bad breath are sexual turnoffs and indicate a lack of respect for your partner. Also, many women are repulsed by certain exotic sexual practices, some of which are dangerous. You should never try to force your mate to do something that makes her uncomfortable. Force and coercion have absolutely no place in lovemaking.

Your satisfaction with your wife is largely a choice you make. You can refuse to compare your wife with some airbrushed model's body pictured in a magazine. Treasure her. Tell her how much you love her body. Use endearing language. Be creative. Call her a bundle of goodies. Make her feel beautiful.

> May you rejoice in the wife of your youth. A loving doe, a
> graceful deer—may her breasts satisfy you always, may you
> ever be captivated by her love (Proverbs 5:18, 19).

Wives, your body belongs to your husband as much as his body belongs to you. God wants you to enjoy the physical aspects of lovemaking and to give pleasure to your mate. You can keep him from seeking satisfaction somewhere else by making your bedroom a garden of earthly delights. Entice him.

Many husbands would be surprised and delighted if their wives would take the initiative in lovemaking now and then. Ban bedroom boredom by trying something new. Keep him coming back for more.

Sometimes newlyweds bring to a marriage certain attitudes about sex which inhibit sexual compatibility.

Julia (not her real name) discovered, shortly after her marriage, that her extremely handsome husband had a strange philosophy of sex. He believed sexual intercourse within marriage was to be reserved strictly for the purpose of conceiving a child. Outside of that, it was wrong. Unfortunately, he had neglected to inform Julia of this until after they had consummated the marriage.

Julia's God-given needs for sexual intimacy went unsatisfied. Three years after their marriage she ran off with another man.

Such a tragedy might have been prevented had the Bible's counsel on sex within marriage been followed, as given in 1 Corinthians 7. This passage clearly indicates that marital lovemaking protects against immorality. Those who advocate abstinence within marriage except for childbearing are unwittingly fostering immorality. Julia is only one example of several real-life illustrations of this I have seen.

Not infrequently it is the wife who brings to the marriage a negative attitude about sex. Sometimes this is inherited from a mother who viewed sex as something to be "endured." Sometimes it is due to religious inhibitions that are not supported by Scripture. Sometimes it is a result of childhood sexual abuse, rape, or incest. For such victims, sex is associated with pain, not pleasure; and this can result in chronic sexual dysfunction.

If you have sexual problems within your marriage, you may need the aid of a good Christian marriage counselor. Sometimes people need more than just prayer. If someone were in an automobile accident and sustained bodily trauma, I would advise them to go to a doctor. I would not say, "Just pray, and it will be all right." So likewise, it is important, when a person has sustained emotional trauma, that he or she receives outside help, whether in the form of a support group or pastoral counseling or therapy.

To underscore this point, here is a letter we received from a listener:

> Your program has helped me to realize that the feelings I am going through even at the age of 34 are normal for anyone who has been a victim of child sexual abuse. I just started counseling the beginning of this year, and yes, counseling does help and I urge anyone who has been sexually abused as a child or even raped to get professional help, because you can't handle it alone.

Sexual hangups can be cured, and sexual sins can be forgiven. The married couple who are attentive and faithful to each other can learn to experience the magic of good sex. How can you enjoy sex without sorrow? Live according to the wisdom of the Bible: If you are single, keep yourself pure. Refuse to participate in sexual expression outside marriage. If you are married, be faithful to your spouse. If you have deprived your spouse, ask God for forgiveness, throw your inhibitions to the wind, and give yourself wholly and gladly to him or her. If both of you will do this, then you will indeed enjoy sex without sorrow.

2

The Good, the Bad, and the Ugly

Hardly anything tastes better than strawberry shortcake. Picture a mountain of berries topped with a big glob of whipped cream! But as wonderful as strawberries are, there is almost nothing worse than biting into a spoiled strawberry.

Sex, like strawberries, can be very good. It can be the mysterious beginning of new life. Sex in marriage can be pure and noble and wonderful.

On the other hand, sex can be bad and ugly. It can alienate lovers, precipitating the end of their relationship. Sex outside of marriage can spread disease and cause emotional and spiritual scarring.

Once when Pastor H.M.S. Richards, Jr. was holding some meetings at a Christian college, an earnest young lady asked him, "What's wrong with having sex with someone you love?" He had a sudden inspiration.

He pointed out the window to the lovely, thick lawn. "What do you think about that lawn out there? Isn't it beautiful?"

"It sure is," she agreed.

"Well, if it's so beautiful," he said, "why not dig up a big plug of it and bring it in here? We could lay it out here on the rug in the lobby and it would make a beautiful addition to the lobby, don't you think?"

"No, no, no," she said, laughing, "that would dirty up the carpet!" And then it hit her.

Sex is like that. God made sex for marriage. In its place, it's beautiful. Outside of marriage, it's dirty.

For some, the Bible's sexual regulations may appear to be severe and repressive. And the church's prohibition of premarital or adulterous sexual activity may seem to be legalistic. Doesn't God want me to be happy? Why did God forbid sexual intercourse outside of marriage? After all, He is the one who made us sexual beings. Does God seek to limit our pleasure, or to enhance it?

Jesus declared that He came to promote life and to make it more abundant and rich (John 10:10). God wants only the best for us. The prohibitions against unrestrained sexual activity were designed by God to protect a wonderful gift.

Within the protective environment of committed, affectionate marriage, sex can be a lifelong joy. Outside of marriage, sexual relations are often reduced to performance. Sex as performance or brief encounter brings momentary pleasure but leaves people cold and empty inside.

I've always admired the insights of C. S. Lewis. Here's something he wrote about sex outside of marriage:

> The inventor of the human machine was telling us that its two halves, the male and the female, were made to be combined together in pairs, not simply on the sexual level, but totally combined. The monstrosity of sexual intercourse outside marriage is that those who indulge in it are trying to isolate one kind of union (the sexual) from all the other kinds of union which were intended to go along with it and make up the total union. The Christian attitude does not mean that there is anything wrong about sexual pleasure, any more than about the pleasure of eating. It means that you must not isolate that pleasure and try to get it by itself, any more than you ought to try to get the pleasures of taste without swallowing and digesting, by chewing things and spitting them out again.

C. S. Lewis died in 1963—long before bulimia and anorexia became household words. Yet Lewis is essentially describing what today is known as the binge/purge syndrome. Today, as in ancient Rome, some people do try to enjoy food without actually digesting it. This kind of behavior can become a life-threatening sickness.

Sex outside of a loving, life-long commitment can be a similar sort of sickness, resulting in spiritual anorexia. It saps a person's emotional and spiritual vitality.

When a doctor orders bed rest, it is not to deprive the patient of pleasure. If he orders more exercise, it is not to impose pain, but to increase well-being. That's why God demands chastity, too. Like a good doctor, He has prescribed sex only within certain limits, because He knows that in the wrong circumstances, it can be poisonous.

If you break God's laws concerning sexual purity, you are actually breaking yourself. It's like trying to break the law of gravity: It's not the law that gets broken; it's you.

In Yosemite National Park, there are signs posted at the top of some of the waterfalls which warn visitors to stay back from the edge and out of the stream. Why? To prevent someone from being swept over the edge.

It's not ignoring the sign that hurts; it's going over the edge. Likewise in the area of sexuality. Extra-marital sexual involvement has negative side effects. The Bible's frequent warnings against fornication and adultery are intended to prevent those tragic consequences.

God's rules arise not out of a negative view of sex but out of an appreciation of the incredible benefits of the real thing. The reason that our government goes to such lengths to prohibit counterfeiting and to seek out and punish those who print counterfeit currency is not because money is bad, but because the real thing is so valuable. Likewise, genuine sex is so good that it is worth protecting.

The human body is full of grace and beauty. Look at your hand. It is a masterpiece of design! Notice the interplay of bone and muscle and tendons; the paradoxical combination of sensitivity and strength; the astonishing perfection of engineering that makes it all work together to stroke a baby's cheek or wield a hammer.

The same God who created the hand created our sexual organs as well. The sexual longings that we feel are an expression of our essential humanity, not our fallen nature. Our sex drive was created by God, and, like all of the rest of His creation, it was very good.

In Genesis 1:27, we read: "So God created man in his own image, in the image of God he created him; male and female he created them."

Our sexual polarity as male and female is part of what it means to be in the image of God. Through the gift of sex, God teaches us the profound value of relationships. Human beings were created to live in companionship. Speaking specifically of Adam before the creation of Eve, God declares, "It is not good for the man to be alone."

After creating mankind as a unity of male and female, God surveyed his creation and declared, "It is very good." God delighted in the differences between Adam and Eve, which resulted in their attraction to each other.

The early Christians created a scandal in their society by their insistence that God had become a human being. To the Greeks, the notion that the great God would actually stoop to such humiliation was unthinkable. Nevertheless, writes John, "The Word became flesh, and lived among us."

If God Himself appeared among us in a human body, then clearly our bodies are not something to be ashamed of or to be grudgingly endured until we can escape them. Lewis Smedes, in his book, *Sex for Christians*, comments on the creation story this way:

> God is not pictured making a soul and wrapping a body around it. . . . Nor is the soul set on earth with a body as baggage for its pilgrimage. To belabor the point, the soul does not drive the body around like an angel driving an

automobile. The biblical story is not about the creation of a soul that possesses or is encumbered by a body; it is about a body that comes alive to God (Lewis B. Smedes, *Sex for Christians*, William B. Eerdmans Publishing Company, 1976], p. 28).

In other words, our bodies are good; God designed us as physical beings. The fact that we are sexual is part of God's plan for us, not a subversion of it. But we are not *merely* sexual beings; we are also spiritual beings. God yearns for spiritual intimacy with us, and sexual immorality interferes with that intimacy. That is why it is such a serious evil:

Flee from sexual immorality. All other sins a man commits are outside his body, but he who sins sexually sins against his own body. Do you not know that your body is a temple of the Holy Spirit, who is in you, whom you have received from God? You are not your own; you were bought at a price. Therefore honor God with your body (1 Corinthians 6:16-20).

Let me say it as plainly as I can. Sexual intercourse between a faithful husband and a loving wife can be one of the peak experiences of life. In a healthy marriage, sexual union is the ultimate expression of intimacy; the physical expression of our passion to know and be known by the beloved. Sexual union can enrich and deepen the emotional, intellectual, and spiritual oneness of a husband and wife. It's magic!

On the other hand, illicit sex may be a source of physical, emotional, and spiritual diseases that wound and destroy. So there are the choices: the Good, the Bad, and the Ugly. The best and the worst. God wants only the very best for you. Why not choose the best?

3

"I've Been Burned, Listen to Me!"

A few years ago *Woman's Day* carried an interesting story about a couple who had their eight-year-old son fingerprinted for safety reasons during a local shopping-center promotion, as a result of a recent media blitz concerning missing children.

Being the independent sort, the boy filled out the blanks in the identification form all by himself—name, eyes, hair, etc. While he was doing this, he was overheard to mutter, "Eyes, yes; sex, *no!*—give me a break, I'm only a kid!"

Unfortunately, kids no longer get a break. Being "only a kid" is no longer protection from the increasingly aggressive onslaught of sexuality on young minds today. According to a *Seventeen* magazine survey of over 2,000 teens, 24 percent of fifteen-year-olds have had sex. By age eighteen, that figure has climbed to 60 percent.

Even religious young people have the idea that if they are not sexually active, they are odd or weird or backward. It's not just hormones that provide sexual incentive. The whole of society—their peers, the media—seems to expect them to give full expression to their adolescent libido.

You may wonder if, in today's culture, there is any need

to talk about the goodness and wonder of sex. After decades of constant bombardment with the new morality in movies, novels, magazines, and on television talk shows, doesn't everyone know that sex is one of the best things in life?

Tragically, the answer is no. The truth is that people are not more sexually fulfilled now than they were decades ago. On the contrary, sexual relations appear to give less pleasure. Today, there is more sexual dysfunction and less desire among married couples than in the so-called "repressive" society of our forefathers.

For many teenagers, sex has been reduced to a troubling, incessant compulsion. "Sex, to us, is like taking vitamins," said one sixteen-year-old girl at Lakewood High in California, "because if you don't have sex, you're not gonna grow up right" (*Los Angeles Times,* March 25, 1993). The physical pleasure they pursue is real enough. And their drives to establish deep bonds with someone, to love and to be loved, are compelling. But for most of them, intimacy remains a hope unfulfilled. An afternoon's liaison cannot give them what they are so desperately seeking.

If you are a working parent, you should know that the most likely time for your teenager's first sexual experience is between 3:00 and 5:00 in the afternoon, after school is out but before you're home from work.

Josh McDowell conducted a survey of teenagers from evangelical churches and discovered they had learned about sex from the following sources: 28 percent learned about sex from friends, 26 percent from movies, 23 percent from classes at school, 23 percent from parents; and, finally, 22 percent checked that they learned about sex from television—keep in mind that they were allowed to check more than one (*Group*, cited in *Teens & Trends*, 12/88-1/89; and *USA Today*, September 22-24, 1989; *Leadership*, Vol. 11, No. 2).

And what are they learning about sex from the movies and from television? Need you ask? Over 90 percent of all the references to sex in daytime soap operas involve partners who are not married to each other (*Psychology Today*, October, 1988). In the movies, sex is excitement. Sex is maturity. Sex is fun. And it never has consequences.

But in real life, it does. Every day, more than 3,000 teenage girls in the U.S. become pregnant. Every day, teen mothers give birth to 1,300 babies. (*Light*, April 1986; *Preaching*, Volume 2, No. 3). And that's the good news! The bad news has to do with venereal diseases, shattered emotions, broken hearts, and AIDS. *Time* magazine (December 9, 1985), points out that teenage mothers are "many times as likely as other women with young children to live below the poverty level. According to one study, only half of those who give birth before age eighteen complete high school (as compared with 96 percent of those who postpone childbearing). On average, they earn half as much money and are far more likely to be dependent on welfare."

Since adolescents see only the glamorous side of illicit sex from the media, here's a few statements from youth who have been there and seen the other side of the matter. You want reality? Then listen to these testimonies taken from Josh McDowell's outstanding book *Why Wait*? Let's hear from those who have been burned.

Premarital sex gave me fear as a gift . . . and shame to wear as a garment. It stole my peace of mind and robbed me of hope in a bright future. Sex smashed my concentration in class to smithereens. My desire for church activities was ground to a pulp. It made crumbs of the trust I had known in Christ . . . and in men and women. Sex gave me a jagged tear in my heart that even now, seven years later, is still healing (*Why Wait*, p. 15).

Here's another sad testimony:

Within two months I gave in, because I had justified the whole thing. Over the next six months, sex became the center of our relationship. Like a cancer, it just took over. At that same time, some new things entered our relationship, things like anger, impatience, jealousy and selfishness. We just couldn't talk any more. We grew very bored with each other and I desperately wanted a change, so I broke up with him (*Why Wait?*, p. 76).

When the sex begins, another writer explains, a couple will stop investing energy into exploring the many facets of each other's personality. With the curiosity and the mystery gone, boredom sets in (*Why Wait?*, p. 291).

Sometimes something even worse than boredom sets in. 1 Kings 13 tells the story of how David's son Amnon fell in love with his half-sister Tamar and forced her to have sex with him. Notice this revealing comment in 1 Kings 13:15 about the emotional after-effects:

Then Amnon hated her with intense hatred. In fact, he hated her more than he had loved her. Amnon said to her, "Get up and get out!"

So, ladies, if you want to keep him, don't let him. Once he's had you, the magic is gone, and he's on to other conquests. When you say no, you will either increase his respect for you and deepen the relationship, or he will leave—and better now than later. If you say yes, you will lose a part of yourself that you can never recover, and your lack of self-control will result in lowered self-esteem and possibly even self-hate.

Lest you think the youth I am quoting are biased toward the Christian viewpoint, let me quote someone who is not: Erica Jong. In *Ms.* magazine (May 1989), she said:

Our society has had a decade and a half of experimentation with random sexual freedom. We have discovered that it is neither so very sexy nor so very free. My generation is disillusioned with sex as a social panacea. We look longingly at the marriages of our parents and grandparents and wonder how on earth they managed to stay best friends for so long—or even worst friends for so long! But at least they had someone to read the newspaper with.

Now let's look at the happy side of the picture. Let me

share with you the testimonies of three who waited. Couple number one:

> God introduced me to Mr. Right and we struggled through a fourteen-month engagement to refrain from premarital sex.... After 3 years of marriage, I have never regretted [it]. ... I firmly believe that waiting until after the "I do's" to experience sex can only enhance the marital relationship. Our doing that established a trust that cannot be equaled (*Why Wait?*, p. 240).

Couple number two:

> Last July, God gave me the most wonderful man in the world to be my husband. . . . On our wedding night, I experienced sex for the first time, and it was with my husband. I wouldn't have wanted to share my first time with anyone else. I had no riches or jewels to offer my husband, but he asked for none. All he wanted was me, and that is just what I had to give him—all of me, untouched, his alone. That meant a great deal, and we both knew it. This was a good enough reason to wait (*Why Wait?*, p. 305).

Finally, couple number three had already blown it, but they repented and decided to abstain:

> My fiancé and I knew we had to get out of our sexual immorality. With God's help we did not engage in sex during the nine months until our wedding. . . . The first time we made love after our wedding, tears of joy streamed down my face. I experienced the true beauty of the sexual relationship as God intended it (*Why Wait?*, p. 317).

Friend, sex is one of God's most beautiful gifts to mankind. Sex is like fire. In a fireplace, it's warm and delightful. Outside the hearth, it's destructive and uncontrollable. I've known many who said to me, "I wish I hadn't done it," but I've never known anyone who waited until they were married and regretted it. For those who are willing to wait, there's a life full of pleasure wrapped up in sex. Don't unwrap the gift too soon. And if you have, it's not too late to repent and let God make you whole again.

4

Truth and Lies About Sex

A young boy was returning from Sunday school, where the Ten Commandments had been the topic of the day. He was puzzled by the seventh commandment, so he asked his father, "Daddy, what does it mean when it says, 'Thou shalt not commit agriculture'?" With hardly a pause, the father replied: "Son, that just means that you're not supposed to plow the other man's field."

Well, if you'll allow me to pursue this fertile metaphor a moment, it seems there's been a lot of strange plowing going on lately. And the crop's in. And the fruit is bitter. If you have any notion of sowing wild oats, I'd like for you to take a few minutes to think about the harvest.

When God made Adam and Eve, He invented sex. He designed sexual union to be the supreme expression of intimacy and love in a life-long commitment. Sexual intimacy was God's gift of pleasure and renewed life.

Something this powerful, this valuable, requires safeguards. In the book of Hebrews, chapter 13, verse 4, we read:

> Marriage should be honored by all, and the marriage bed kept pure, for God will judge the adulterer and all the sexually immoral.

Satan always seeks to take that which is holy and make

it vile. Have you ever noticed that profanity is language about God or about sex—two holy things? Satan has always sought to drag down the holy.

During the sixties, in particular, sexual looseness became a social revolution. In the November 6, 1970, issue of *Life* magazine a reputed expert in human sexuality declared, "In the first place, we must rid our minds of the idea that there are any special moral rules for sexual behavior. Sexual pleasure is never wrong."

In the almost three decades since the explosion of voices advocating free love, this revolution has touched every segment of society. For decades, prominent personalities have ridiculed the Bible's sexual ethic. Sex is for fun, they say, not for keeps. They have assured us that following their advice would lead to greater self-fulfillment and happiness.

In recent years, we have seen the fruit of their counsel.

Our society is being destroyed by the collapse of families in an epidemic of divorce. Every value is in decline—honesty, hard work, integrity, temperance, public service. Strong young bodies are being ruined by sexually transmitted diseases. Some of these diseases can be treated with a fair degree of success. But others, like chlamydia and AIDS, have inescapable consequences. Chlamydia, a burgeoning venereal disease, leads to lifelong sterility in 25 percent of the girls who contract it. AIDS kills.

A fourteen-year-old girl who has been made sterile for life by chlamydia is not free. The twenty-five-year-old graduate student dying with AIDS becomes a stranger to pleasure. The young wife, whose union with her husband is unsettled by the haunting memories of her teenage sexual adventures, finds that her past has become a ball and chain on her mind. These children of God are tasting the bitter truth that disobedience to God's commands leads to slavery and death.

Genuine freedom comes only by living in voluntary

submission to certain restrictions. A string of violin wire lying unstrung on the table is free to twist and turn in any direction, but it is not free to make beautiful music. Only when its movement is severely restricted can it do that.

If you want your life to make beautiful music, you have to choose your freedoms with care. If you want to be free to live, you are not free to jump out of a tenth-story window and experience the joys of flight. If you want to have the uncanny freedom, on the uneven parallel bars, of an Olympic medalist, or the keyboard freedom of a world-class pianist, then you are not free to spend your evenings partying.

If you really want to have a happy marriage and a bright future, you are not free to experiment sexually. Premature freedom can lead to bondage of the worst sort.

A life without self-control is destined for desolation. Only an infant wants what he wants when he wants it; mature people learn to control their appetites. We cannot have freedom without responsibility. I like the way British statesman Edmund Burke demolished this myth: "Men," he writes,

> are qualified for civil liberty in exact proportion to their disposition to put moral chains on their own appetites. Society cannot exist unless a controlling power upon will and appetite be placed somewhere, and the less of it there is within, the more there is without. It is ordained in the eternal constitution of things that men of intemperate minds cannot be free. Their passions forge their fetters.

Speaking of fetters, even worse than the diseases of the body mentioned earlier is the desolation of soul that comes with promiscuity.

In his book, *No Wonder They Call Him the Savior*, Max Lucado tells the sad story of Judith Bucknell. She was stabbed and strangled on a steamy June evening in 1980. It was discovered that she kept a diary, and her diary is a painful epitaph to a lonely life. In her diary Judith speaks with wistful, weary, yearning voice. At age thirty-eight, a successful secretary, her diary is filled with entries like this one: "Where are the men with the flowers and champagne and music? Where are the men who call and ask for a genuine, actual date? Where are the men who would like to share more than my bed, my booze, my food. . . . I would like to have in my life, once before I pass through my life, the kind of sexual relationship which is part of a loving relationship."

She never did. Judy was not a prostitute. She was not on drugs or on welfare. She never went to jail. She was not a social outcast. She was respectable. She hosted parties. She wore designer clothes and had an apartment that overlooked the bay. And she was very lonely. "I see people together and I'm so jealous I want to throw up. What about me! What about me!" Though she had many lovers, she had little love. "Who is going to love Judy Bucknell?" the diary continues. "I feel so old. Unloved. Unwanted. Abandoned. Used up. I want to cry and sleep forever."

Superficial intimacies do not cure loneliness; they only deepen it.

Edna St. Vincent Millay made the same discovery. She had a wonderful gift of poetry. But she lived an immoral life. Oh, it was great while it lasted:

My candle burns at both ends;
     It will not last the night;
But, ah, my foes, and, oh, my friends—
     It gives a lovely light.

Inevitably, the light went out. Notice how she described her loss as she put her feelings into rhyme one rainy night:

What lips my lips have kissed, and where, and why,
     I have forgotten, and what arms have lain
Under my head till morning; but the rain
     Is full of ghosts tonight, that tap and sigh
Upon the glass and listen for reply;
     And in my heart there stirs a quiet pain
For unremembered lads that not again
     Will turn to me at midnight with a cry.

Thus in the winter stands the lonely tree,
 Nor knows what birds have vanished one by one,
Yet knows its boughs more silent than before:
 I cannot say what loves have come and gone;
I only know that summer sang in me
 A little while, that in me sings no more.

Friend, if you are in the spring of your life, and you are living in immorality, let me assure you that the summer of your life will be short and the winter very dark. "I only know that summer sang in me a little while, that in me sings no more." And no wonder. For the Bible says, "A woman who lives for pleasure is dead even while she lives" (1 Timothy 5:6). The same goes for men.

In real life, promiscuity brings emptiness. What a different picture from the Hollywood myth of sex as parlor sport, where love is reduced to lust and chastity is portrayed as churlishness. With vivid colors and lush music, the silver screen glamorizes the blissful coupling of lithe bodies in rapturous embrace. Ah, the joys of free sex! But we are never shown the end result: the drab gray of a shriveled soul.

There is no contest between the beauty of sexual intimacy in marriage and the transitory, desolating pleasures of fornication or adultery. God's way is better.

Our culture has made a god of uninhibited sex. The prophets of this god promise total freedom and unending bliss. But they lie. The promises of the sexual revolution have proven false. The pleasure is at best fleeting. Only God can provide everlasting joy. He gives a sense of purpose and meaning in life that external circumstances cannot take away. He will provide this kind of richness for all who will open their lives to His grace.

We have a choice: the way of promiscuity, titillation, disease, and death. Or the way of sexual purity, intimacy, love, and freedom.

5

The Great Safe Sex Boondoggle

I was standing near the prescription counter at the local pharmacy awaiting my doctor's refill for post-surgical pain pills when I overheard two teenaged girls debating in hushed tones behind me in the next aisle. One girl asked the other if she and her boyfriend used condoms. "No," she muttered, "we don't buy them because it's too embarrassing to go up to the counter with them! It's like we're announcing we're going to have sex tonight!"

This chapter is about one of the great tragedies of our times: the myth of safe sex. It's a sensitive subject; not the sort of presentation I would recommend for small children. But I am going to be very explicit about the problems because I care about kids.

Sex is not "safe" for many reasons. It is emotionally intense. Outside of marriage, it uses up people; it ruins lives; there is nothing safe about it. But in this chapter we will focus only on the issue of physical safety.

What does "safe sex" mean? Bluntly stated, "safe sex" means sex using a condom. Current educational policy assumes that kids are going to experiment with sex no matter what. Since everybody's doing it, we may as well face facts and provide some safeguards, such as free condoms.

Does making condoms readily available to young people help reduce teenage pregnancy and the spread of disease? Or does it have the opposite effect? Let's look at the evidence.

Telling a kid "If you're gonna have sex, use a condom" is like telling a kid "If you're gonna drag-race, wear your seatbelt." You might as well tell a kid, "If you're gonna play Russian roulette, make sure there's only one bullet in the chamber."

Anyone who says things like this to teenagers is foolishly ignorant of the way human nature works. Kids are experts at reading between the lines. Recommending condom usage conveys the idea that "safe sex" is possible, that everybody's doing it, and that it's okay. Such counsel ruins lives by giving kids implicit permission to practice self-destructive behavior.

Thomas Sowell, in his book *Inside American Education* (The Free Press, 1993), cites studies indicating that teen pregnancy rates were declining for over a decade before sex education programs were widely implemented in the 1970s but then rose sharply along with increased federal funding for those programs. The more money the government spends to teach kids about sex, the more promiscuous the kids become.

Since 1970, the government has spent several billion dollars to promote so-called "safe sex." Today most youth know the basic facts of reproduction and birth control. But has this knowledge resulted in prudent behavior?

The conversation I overheard in the drug store gives a strong clue. The answer is no. Large-scale surveys of college students by Baldwin and Baldwin at the University of California found that less than 20 percent of sexually active women and men reported using condoms 75 percent of the time or more (*Newsweek*, December 9, 1991, p. 54). This study and others (Cheryl D. Hayes, 1987; William D. Mosher and James W. MacNally, 1991; etc.) indicate that *most teenagers and college students engage in sex with no protection most of the time.*

Discouraging. Distressing. Safe sex programs are a dismal failure. We cannot expect young people to be both promiscuous and responsible.

What's even more alarming is this: Even if all teenagers conscientiously used condoms, they would still be at risk, because condoms are not reliable.

One study by the Centers for Disease Control and Prevention in Atlanta found that 12 percent to 21 percent of new, fresh-from-the-manufacturer condoms available in this country had unacceptable rates of leakage ("Condoms for Prevention of Sexually Transmitted Diseases," *Morbidity and Mortality Weekly Report*, 37:133, 1988). A significant percentage of condoms have five-micron holes in them. A five-micron hole is invisible without a microscope, but it is fifty times larger than the AIDS virus.

But this is just the beginning of the trouble with condoms. After they've been made, condoms can be damaged in several ways. They are damaged by exposure over several days to air containing ozone at levels frequently found in Southern California. Condoms are *drastically* damaged by exposure to petroleum-based or oil-based lubricants such as baby oil, vaseline, or corn oil. They are also damaged when stored at temperatures that exceed 100 degrees. Since the temperature inside an enclosed car on a hot day can reach 160 degrees, condoms stored in glove compartments are unreliable. Wait—it gets worse. Condoms are transported to stores in trucks which are not temperature controlled. The heat in these trucks can cause invisible damage to the condoms inside their sealed packages.

New York City officials announced on November 27, 1990, that they had recalled 750,000 condoms that had been distributed to teenage pregnancy and AIDS groups due to a possibility of leakage. No word was given as to how many were no longer available for recall.

It appears that the ship of safe sex has sprung a leak!

The Alan Guttmacher Institute in New York is a well-known human sexuality research facility. They discovered that the number of pregnancies likely to occur in 100 married couples using condoms as a method of birth control is fourteen. Among young, unmarried minority women the failure rate for condoms is not 14 percent but 36 percent (Elise F. Jones and Nacqueline Darroch Forrest, "Contraceptive Failure in the United States: Revised Estimates from the 1982 National Survey of Family Growth," *Family Planning Perspectives* 21 [May/June 1989], p. 105).

Now *think:* it is possible for a girl to get pregnant only about three days out of the month, yet it is possible to catch the AIDS virus thirty days out of the month. And the AIDS virus is 450 times smaller than human sperm. So if condoms have a 14-to-36 percent failure rate in preventing pregnancy, they must have a much *higher* failure rate in preventing AIDS. Clearly it is foolhardy to trust a condom for protection from AIDS.

The implications of this are staggering. Human nature being what it is, the unintended consequences of the "safe sex" philosophy far outweigh the intended consequences—so much so that condom advocacy has become a major contributor to the explosion of teenage pregnancies and the epidemic of sexually transmitted diseases. *In a manner of speaking, condoms facilitate the spread of AIDS!*

Let's look at an actual test case. In 1989, Adams City High in Commerce, Colorado, became one of the first public schools in the nation to distribute condoms to students. The school has also adopted a teen parenting program. So by now we would expect teen pregnancies to have dropped significantly, right? *Wrong!* The birth rate at the school has climbed to 31 percent above the national average of 58 births per 1000 students. In the 1991-92 school year at Adams City High, there were 100 pregnancies, as compared to only 76 the year before (*EP News Service*, July 24, 1992, p. 10).

The "safe sex" campaign is a national tragedy. Thousands of teenagers are ruining their lives because of the influence of so-called safe sex programs—programs that were intended to protect them. No amount of money spent on educational programs can offset the loss of high ideals on a young person's morals.

But there is a better way. Kids *do* respond positively to strong abstinence messages. Kids want limits. They respect them and thrive under them, even as they buck them. They want to know how to abstain without losing their friends. In fact, surveys indicate that the sex information teenage girls want most is how to say no without hurting feelings. Teaching total abstinence offers the greatest hope of preventing unwanted pregnancies and sexual diseases. Many successful programs are using this philosophy today.

Geoffrey Canada teaches karate in Harlem. In return for his teaching, he demands a strict standard of moral behavior. His students stay in school. They don't break the law. And they don't have children out of wedlock. There has not been a single pregnancy in ten years (Joe Klein, "How About a Swift Kick?" *Newsweek*, July 26, 1993, p. 30).

Marion Howard originated a program at Emory University for eighth-grade inner-city youngsters, called Postponing Sexual Involvement. The program advocates saving sex for marriage. Those who have been through her program report five times less sexual activity than those who have not been through the program. Dr. Phyllis Magrab and Elayne Bennett, M.Ed., in their program called Best Friends, have now had more than five hundred young people involved in their program, with only one pregnancy on the part of one young girl who had left the program (*Sexual Health Update*, May, 1993, Vol 1., No. 3; published by Medical Institute for Sexual Health [P.O. Box 4919, Austin, TX 78765]).

In some schools today, the students themselves are waking up and rebelling against the bankrupt philosophy that tells them they are merely highly advanced animals. There are student groups that are demanding courses that stress abstinence. Perhaps a new day is coming, and with God's grace and your help, it will come sooner.

Several denominations and Christian organizations are sponsoring the "True Love Waits" campaign, which asks teens to sign the following chastity pledge: "Believing that true love waits, I make a commitment to God, myself, my family, those I date, my future mate and my future children, to be sexually pure until the day I enter a covenant marriage relationship." So far, hundreds of thousands of kids have signed.

Our children need bold, grand ideals. They need to know that we prize chastity, that we do not accept promiscuity, and that everyone is NOT doing it. In fact, nearly two-thirds of all high school females under eighteen are virgins (U.S. Department of Health and Human Services, National Centers for Health Statistics, Centers for Disease Control and Prevention, "Percent of Women 15-19 Years of Age Who are Sexually Experienced, by Race, Age, and Marital Status: United States, 1988," *National Survey of Family Growth*), and of the high achievers in American high schools, three fourths are virgins (Josh McDowell, *The Myths of Sex Education* [Thomas Nelson, 1990], pp. 29, 31).

We must stop disseminating the "safe sex" myth before we turn another generation of children into sacrificial lambs on the altar of modern morality. We cannot throw up our hands in despair and say, "Today's young people have no morals." Instead, we need to lovingly educate our young people. Let's tell them that virginity is worth fighting for; that marriage is worth waiting for. Let's assure them that even if they have stumbled into sexual sin, they can be forgiven and become pure and have a fulfilling, lifelong relationship with a companion they really love.

6

We're Committed, So Why Wait?

The number of unmarried American couples who are living together today is approaching three million. More than half of all couples live together before marriage. At first glance this seems like a good idea. Why not try out a relationship before making a commitment which may cost thousands of dollars to get out of? After all, we wouldn't buy a new suit of clothes before trying it on, would we?

There is no question that a sexual relationship between two unmarried but committed partners is very different from a lifestyle of promiscuity. What are the chances of long-term success in such a relationship?

For ten years Dr. Nancy Moore Clatworthy, associate professor of sociology at Ohio State University, studied the phenomenon of unmarried couples living together. When she began studying this, she was predisposed to favor the practice. The couples reported that it was wonderful, and she believed them. It seemed like a logical step in courtship to help couples get to know one another.

But her research involving hundreds of couples living together changed her mind. She found that, when it came to happiness, respect, and adjustment, "Couples who lived together before their marriage had more problems than

31

couples who married first. In every area, these couples disagreed more often."

Moreover, there was a problem with commitment. Knowing that something is temporary affects the degree of commitment to it. So unmarried couples are less than wholehearted in working to protect the relationship. As a result, most such couples break up in the end. "Practice doesn't make perfect," she says. Statistically, you are much better off marrying than living together.

Other studies back up the findings of Clatworthy. A 1983 study by the National Council on Family Relations also found that couples who live together before marriage are less happy in their marriages.

Forty percent of these live-in couples break up before marriage. Of the rest that go on to get married, you might expect that the divorce rate would be quite a bit lower than average. After all, the incompatible couples have already split, so that leaves only compatible couples, right? Wrong. *About three out of four of those marriages end in divorce.* Put another way, couples who live together before marrying have nearly an 80 percent higher divorce rate than those who do not, according to a recent National Bureau of Economic Research survey (*Single Adult Ministries Journal*, July-August, 1988; in *Leadership*, Vol. 10, No. 2).

The bottom line is that out of 100 trial marriages, only fifteen form lasting marriages. Let me repeat that. If you live with your lover before marriage, your chances of a strong, lasting marriage are only 15 percent, or three out of twenty. Those are terrible odds.

Let's look at some reasons why this is true.

One of the essential ingredients in a happy marriage is mutual trust and respect. Men in particular have a need to be looked up to, respected, and admired. But do women respect men who cannot control themselves sexually? No. For this reason it is a common pattern among married couples who engage in premarital sex for the wife eventually to end up wearing the pants in the family.

So gentlemen, if you want the admiration and respect of your wife, demonstrate some self-control.

Ladies, you too get little respect if you're a live-in. In any given year during the 1980s, one out of every thousand wives was assaulted by her husband. Tragic. But among unmarried couples living together, sixty-six out of every thousand women were assaulted by their lovers. That's one out of fifteen. Talk about no respect!

Premarital chastity not only makes for mutual respect, it generates trust, because it stands to reason that those who were able to resist sex with their partner before marriage will be more likely to resist the advances of all others after marriage. On the other hand, whenever I find a marriage where one spouse is extremely jealous and suspicious of the other, the couple almost always has a history of premarital sex.

Self-denial and self-control are an important aspect of marriage. Believe me, you do not want to get married to someone who has no self-control and is not willing to deny himself or herself for the greater good of the family. How can you weed out such prospects? The answer is obvious, isn't it? Premarital chastity is a good test to see whether two people are mature enough to get married.

Self-control and self-discipline lead to self-respect. So think of foregoing sex during your engagement in the same way you might think of running the marathon or learning a new language. It is a significant achievement which will always bring you quiet satisfaction.

Loving someone unconditionally is hard work, but it pays rich dividends. Unfortunately, love without reservation is not possible in a live-in situation. Unreserved love means unqualified commitment. Commitment is something a trial marriage does not have. In fact, because there has been no verbal commitment to monogamy, a great deal of cheating goes on in most live-in situations.

For a couple living together but not married, there is a constant, subtle evaluation process going on. Is he or she really good enough to spend the rest of my life with? Are we really compatible? Is this person I'm living with more fun, more satisfying than anyone else I could be with?

In even the best trial marriage, the partners are saying, "I like you and think I might want to live with you for a long time, maybe forever; but I'm not yet ready to promise. I want to keep my options open."

If you are dating and your partner is pressing you to agree to move in together, the only safe response is to say: "I can understand your feelings, and I accept them. *However, until you give me all of yourself, you don't get all of me.*" Women, especially, if you want to keep your lover forever, don't give him everything until he is man enough to make it legal. After all, you're the one who is taking the greatest risk. The bare facts are that if he dumps you, you are more likely to spend the rest of your life alone than he is. He is the one with the greatest earning power; but you are the one most likely to end up caring for a fatherless child.

Experimenting sexually is not like jumping into a pool to test the water. When you jump into an icy swimming pool, you climb out the same person you were when you went in. A few minutes of shivering and you're back where you were. But you can't do that sexually. When you jump into bed with someone, barring a miracle, you are never the same again (to find out why, see the next chapter).

So testing the waters sexually is hazardous. Actually, engagement is the time for testing the waters; a time to explore in depth the issues that will affect the future through long discussions—which would rapidly be short-circuited by sex. A deep, long-lasting relationship is established by progressing through certain steps in the right order: first the intellectual, then the emotional and spiritual, then the physical. If you bypass the earlier stages and move too quickly to the physical, genuine intimacy never develops. You may never come to really know each other as whole persons with memories and values and dreams. This risk of aborting the development of intimacy is too great a risk to take if you really love someone.

In my counseling of engaged couples, I now insist they make a pledge to abstain from intercourse until their wedding night—or I simply won't perform the marriage. After the wedding, they are delighted with the results!

In 1993, Dear Abby, after receiving a letter from a girl who had moved in with an abusive boyfriend and was glad she found him out before marriage, changed her longtime position on this issue. Abby decided that maybe it wasn't such a bad idea after all to test the waters by cohabiting. As a result, she was deluged with letters to the contrary and quickly admitted that this was perhaps some of the worst advice she had ever given. One writer cited a recent study covering twenty-three years by Axinn and Thornton of the University of Chicago and the University of Michigan. The study found that "the possibility of cohabitation weakens a commitment to marriage as an institution" and "produces attitudes and values that increase the probability of divorce." (Dear Abby, Friday, April 2, 1993).

Given the proven negative consequences of sexual intimacy before marriage, why would anyone experiment with sex outside of marriage? Some do it because they simply can't wait. Others do it because they think they love each other, and sexual union is a natural goal of a love relationship between a man and woman. Most aren't familiar with the research that indicates the problems with it.

But responsible lovers will want to do whatever it takes to develop the richest, most joyous relationship possible. And, as we have seen, even modern science is telling us that one of the key ingredients of that kind of relationship is reserving sexual intimacy until after marriage. Christian marriage is a total commitment of the total person for total life. That kind of a relationship is worth waiting for.

7

The Pleasure Bond

Once, early in our marriage, my wife burned a hole in my dress pants. The iron was too hot. Fortunately, we found a new pair a few days later that exactly matched the suit coat. But we learned the hard way that when too much electricity flows through an iron it will burn a rather permanent hole in whatever material it touches.

The human memory works in somewhat the same way. Events associated with weak emotions make weak impressions, and events associated with strong emotions make strong impression. The more psychic "electricity," the more indelible the memory. The most vivid memories are those made under intense passion. When we have an emotional high, it's as if there is an indelible magic marker that writes on the brain cells, and the event associated with that emotion is forever imprinted in the memory.

For this reason, most people never forget their early sexual experiences. They are burned into the memory forever.

This has some interesting implications for human relationships. These implications have been explored by Donald M. Joy, Ph.D., a professor at Asbury Theological Seminary in Kentucky, in his books *Bonding, Relationships in the Image of God*, and *Re-Bonding, Preventing and Restoring Damaged Relationships*. Much of the material in this chapter is gleaned from interviews with Dr. Joy.

If two people share some sort of emotionally moving experience, a bond is formed between them. The strength of the bond depends upon the intensity of the experience. Milder forms of bonding occur, for example, when two people share a pleasant meal together; table fellowship results in friendship.

Joy, citing Desmond Morris, suggests that there is a twelve-step process, common to all cultures, that leads to an exclusive life-long bond between a man and a woman.

1. Eye to person
2. Eye to eye
3. Voice to voice
4. Hand to hand
5. Arm to shoulder
6. Arm to waist
7. Face to face
8. Head to head
9. Hand to body (excluding genitals)
10. Mouth to breast
11. Hand to genital
12. Genital to genital

It is important that this process not be rushed, because when steps are skipped, the bond that is formed tends to be imperfect. The complete pair-bonding progression moves the partners through a series of emotional plateaus. The final step makes the bond permanent and results in a lifelong "cleaving" to each other in the Genesis sense.

A person's first sexual experience can be the most intense emotional experience of his or her life, forming a powerful pleasure bond with his or her partner. This bond—the mental association between the pleasure and the partner with whom it was experienced—was intended by God to cement two married people together for life.

Dr. Harold Shryock reports in his book *On Becoming a*

Man how this worked in his marriage. He was a virgin on his wedding day. Immediately after the wedding he had some misgivings and doubts. Had he made the right decision to think that he could stay married to this woman forever? Was she really the right one? However, after their first sexual encounter, he experienced a powerful conviction—on a deeper level than that of the intellect—that this woman was the only person he could ever love. His heart was fused with hers; they became soul mates.

That is the way God intended sex within marriage to work. That's the good news. Here's the bad news: It only works that way the first time. Most people only get one chance to form that perfect bond. Human beings simply are not wired for multiple intimate relationships. When two non-virgins are married, the pleasure bond that is formed is usually imperfect or missing. The bonding mechanism can also be damaged by a long history of masturbation, which amounts to sex with multiple imaginary partners.

Here's what happens when bonding has occurred with more than one person. First of all, in marriage, the ghost of that early partner will always haunt the bedroom. Sex will be at least a three-party affair: husband, wife, and the memories of other lovers.

When a person has had more than five or so sexual partners, something worse happens: he or she loses the ability to bond at all. There is no more capacity for an exclusive life-long relationship, for a promiscuous person is incapable of forming deep, lasting emotional bonds. *Once someone has gone through the bonding process too many times, the glue wears out.*

Not only do people who have had multiple sexual partners tend to lose their capacity to bond; they also lose their self-esteem. They tend to regard others as mere objects, and themselves as well. They feel empty and worthless. Unfortunately, this emotional devastation is not something that heals easily or quickly. Usually such people can find healing only with professional therapy or group support. They might want to investigate a support group for sexually dependent people, such as Sexual Addicts Anonymous (SAA), Sexaholics Anonymous (SA), or Sex and Love Addicts Anonymous (SLAA), or some network of healing set up by a local congregation.

In today's culture, people tend to establish substantial bonds with too many partners. Sometimes this can happen almost inadvertently. Marriages can be lost because of bonds being formed in the workplace. When we have emotion-charged experiences with other people, especially when we share a deep hurt, a bond is formed. Frequently people become very attached once they've listened to each other's tragedy or have passed through a crisis together.

However, such bonding is less likely to form unless there is substantial privacy. One safeguard is to avoid being alone with a person of the opposite sex. We are less vulnerable in community. For this reason, group dating is preferable for teenagers. In a group or congregation, we can safely express a lot of affection and listen to confession without danger. But when we do this behind closed doors, it is dangerous. All counselors and therapists are at risk because they traffic in emotion-laden material. They are very vulnerable to forming alien bonds.

Sometimes alien bonds are formed inadvertently, even when one is being careful. In that case, a person must have a strong moral code to fall back on.

Bill was the Bible teacher at a Christian high school. He was married to a beautiful woman and had three children. But he was having trouble at home. He felt like his wife, Susan, would never really understand him. He felt lonely and isolated, despite being married. There was a female staff member at the school who, it seemed to him, was everything Susan was not. This woman was intellectually stimulating. She was spiritually passionate. Conversation with her was like a long, cold drink of water on a scorching August afternoon.

Together with other faculty members, they went for a day in the mountains. The group was startled by a blizzard. Bill and several others began to show signs of hypothermia. Part of the time, the only way the group could stay together was by holding hands in a long chain. When they finally reached their cars at the trail head, they were emotionally and physically exhausted. Bill drove his friend to her house, walked her to the door, then almost before he knew what was happening, they were kissing.

They said goodnight and Bill left—his heart racing. As he drove home, his conscience woke up. What had he done?

Without intending to, Bill had formed an emotional bond with this woman because of their physical contact during a period of shared emotional intensity.

For weeks, he wrestled with the new feelings that the afternoon on the mountain and the kiss at the door had set ablaze in his heart. This woman was so desirable. On the other hand, the words of his marriage vows pounded in his head: "Keep thee only unto her."

After a long talk with a pastor friend, he summoned the courage to renounce the new affection. He renewed his determination to cherish his wife. Today, he and Susan have enriched their marriage and discovered new joy together. They are learning afresh the meaning of unconditional love.

Notice that it was the law that woke Bill up to his danger. The Ten Commandments thundered, "Thou shalt not commit adultery," and the Holy Spirit aroused his conscience and awakened him to the danger of an affair.

Christians have sometimes allowed the wonderful truth that we are saved by grace through faith to obscure the fact that the law has a legitimate function in the Christian life. "By the law is the knowledge of sin." It warns us off forbidden ground. As long as we heed its warning, we remain free. James 2:12 says, "Speak and act as those who are going to be judged by the law that gives freedom. . ."

How is it that the law gives freedom?

Bill's story is a prime illustration. The law can prevent the potential destruction of a marriage by sin. It can keep us free from the enslaving consequences of infidelity.

Lifelong fidelity to one mate? Isn't that a terribly old-fashioned idea? Does anyone really believe that anymore?

Harvard professor Robert Coles wrote a book with Jeff Stokes called *Sex and the American Teenager*. He studied over a thousand families who subscribed to *Rolling Stone* magazine. He found that the teenage children of these families were more conservative in their sexual appetites and behavior than their parents were at a comparable age. They were looking for one exclusive life-long relationship, and they tended to believe that their first love was the one. When they lost that relationship, the boys grieved longer than the girls did over the loss of that first love. We have enormously underrated men and their capacity to grieve deeply.

Amazingly, most emotionally healthy teenagers do share this ideal of exclusive, monogamous love. Most hope that somewhere there's one person who can share all their secrets; with whom they can share a lifetime of fulfillment and trust. If you have that dream, hang on to it.

On their fiftieth wedding anniversary, Mr. and Mrs. Henry Ford attended a celebration in their honor. The ever-present reporters asked Ford, "To what do you attribute your successful marriage, Mr. Ford?" His answer: "The formula is the same as I used to make a successful car. Stick to one model."

If you want the best for your marriage, then avoid premature bonding. Broken bonds mean broken hearts. Don't go too far up the twelve-step ladder of intimacy with anyone you don't want to permanontly bond with. Keep the deep well-springs of your heart free for the one you want to love forever. You'll never regret it.

8

The Enticing Shame

Dear Pastor Melashenko,

By the time I was 18 years old I was a drug addict and drunk. I used any kind of drug I could get—you name it, I did it. But Jesus Christ was and is so good and merciful, He delivered me from all these things.

There is still one thing that has got a hold on me . . . pornography. It started when I was a very young boy at the age of eight years old. As I grew older it got worse than any drug that I had ever taken. It has been more addictive than anything I have ever done. I know that Jesus can deliver. Please pray for me.

Pornography is a monster. It victimizes women by encouraging violent lust in men. It victimizes children by compelling them into grotesque sexual activities which are filmed and photographed for the sick pleasure of wicked men. It victimizes teenage boys and young men by luring them into soul- and body-destroying sexual addiction. For some men, like Ted Bundy or Jeffrey Dahmer, whose criminal careers began with pornography, there is no stopping place on the road to the lowest depths of hell.

No one is invulnerable. Peter was the son of a seminary professor. He and his wife lived in New York City, where he was attending graduate school in one of the arts. His commute to school took him through Times Square. Peter found himself increasingly tantalized by the pornography advertised so garishly on the fronts of the triple-X-rated cinemas and peep shows that are clustered on 42nd Street near 8th Avenue. Finally, he went inside.

He excused this first excursion, saying, "I need to know what this is all about. How can you condemn something unless you really know what is going on?" When a friend protested that he was playing with fire, Peter laughed him off. "Hey, lighten up. Nothing bad's going to happen. I was just checking it out."

A couple of years elapsed before Peter visited his friend, a pastor, at his new home on Long Island. They talked about Peter's broken marriage. Then during several hours of rambling, disjointed conversation, Peter slowly spilled the story of his affair with a teenage boy. The most astounding revelation was not that Peter had stooped so low as to seduce a teenager, but that Peter showed no awareness of the heinousness of what he had done. Peter had no remorse for his deed; he was angry at the boy's parents for breaking up their liaison.

How far he had fallen! And it started with pornography.

How we fall into sin is always somewhat mysterious. We are all made differently. Our life histories are different. But there are certain predictable patterns. One of those patterns is the way sexual promiscuity develops: It often begins with pornography.

In the early seventies, there was a furious debate in the United States over whether or not pornography was harmful. The debate was fueled by the report of a presidential commission which had been established to study the issue. The commission's report declared that pornography, whatever its morality or immorality, appeared to have no negative social impact. It did not lead to increased crime or increased promiscuous sexual behavior.

Advocates of so-called sexual freedom hailed the report as proof that old-fashioned Christian prohibitions on pornography and sexual looseness were merely vestiges of medieval superstition. The vanguard of the sexual revolution declared we had entered a new era of unrestrained self-expression and fulfillment.

What the major media failed to report was that there was a minority report which flatly contradicted the views of the majority on the commission. The minority report cited reference after reference in the commission's own documentation which gave lie to the majority report. Studies that supposedly demonstrated the harmlessness of pornography were of very questionable validity. Studies which strongly suggested the dangers of pornography had simply been ignored by the majority.

In the twenty years since the commission issued its reports, it has become obvious that the minority was right. Nowadays a wide spectrum of thinkers opposes the toxicity of pornography—Christians and feminists, law enforcement officials and psychologists, political conservatives and civil rights advocates.

Pornography is in itself an assault on the humanity and dignity of women. It incites its viewers, mostly men, to violence against women and to sexual perversion. Even worse is the fact that increasingly, it victimizes children!

Sexual impurity that involves children, such as pornography and incest, comes under a most severe curse:

> If anyone causes one of these little ones who believe in me to sin, it would be better for him to have a large millstone hung around his neck and to be drowned in the depths of the sea. Woe to the world because of the things that cause people to sin! Such things must come, but woe to the man through whom they come! (Matthew 18:6, 7).

Pornography warps people—the producers, the actors and models, and the viewers. Sometimes a single exposure to pornography may be enough to trigger a powerful sexual addiction.

Very recently, after the manuscript of this book was

mostly finished, we received the following letter at the Voice of Prophecy in response to a radio program we had done on pornography. It is reproduced here, with slight editing, by permission of the writer:

I can testify to the need to get away from the grip of pornography. My addiction started long before I came to know the Lord.

At age 10, an older brother threw a *Playboy* magazine at me and told me to go masturbate in the bathroom. This was the start of a long, drawn-out defeat that landed me in prison because I chose to ignore it and try to deal with it myself. This addiction is one that doesn't just stop at magazines. They only kindled the fire.

As I became older, I started to become sexually active or abusive, whichever the case may be. This would be about age 12.

By the time I was 15, I had a girlfriend who was about 20 years old.

At age 19, I was sent to prison for 6 months for theft and burglary charges. It was just before this I came to know the Lord. At this time I was living with a girl of 17 whom I was going to marry. This relationship was destroyed because of my prison time.

I had several homosexual encounters at different times, the first of which happened in the county jail before going to prison. I was coerced and raped in the jail.

Although I knew the Lord and was learning His word daily, I still was tormented by my addiction. At this point, I began to wrestle with it, and what a battle! The problems rose and fell, like a tide, with my spirituality. By age 22, I married, and am happy that the Lord gave me the wife I now have, for we are still together.

For a while after we married, things seemed to go better, but then we moved away from the area—2,100 miles away.

Soon, the lack of spiritual input led me back to the addiction of the flesh. I found myself in strip bars blowing half my paycheck on women to dance for me. Also, I met a girl and proceeded to have an affair over a period of a year, which nearly ended my marriage. And there were others, too.

We moved back to Oregon to save our marriage. Even after getting back, I still struggled going to strip bars. At this time, I started getting into XXX-rated home videos. This still wasn't enough to satisfy my addiction. I wanted more and more.

My daughter (from my fiancee before going to prison the first time) was with her mother in Tacoma, Washington. When I would go to visit her, I started to go to bath houses and massage parlors and more exotic strip joints. This only created a deeper craving for more sex. Not being able to find a release, my addiction turned toward a girl in the church who was a very close friend of the family. My abuse of her was a brief encounter; nevertheless, it was what brought me to the point of facing my addiction.

I thank God for stopping me before it went beyond touching. I couldn't live with what I had done, so I went to the pastor of the church I had been attending for over 12 years.

The unfortunate thing was it was his granddaughter. I tried to confide in him, which proved futile, as he soon quit talking to me. I tried talking to another elder who soon deserted me after I turned myself in to the police. Only two people in the church came to see me after that, though all had opportunity.

One other fellow and his wife came forward to speak on my behalf in court and was soon feeling public ridicule. The mother of the child wrote several letters to the local paper naming the people who would come forward for me. And all of them felt the heat of the community and neglect.

My family, wife, and kids felt the anger of the community to the point that they had to move.

The point I'm trying to make is, yes, I am an offender; yes, I did wrong; but now not only do I suffer, so does my family. This addiction is progressive, and its roots started as a child reading a book out of curiosity, and developed into a nightmare 22 years later.

Now the world wants nothing to do with the likes of me or anyone who supports me. I've tried to receive counseling several times and suffered abuse and neglect because of it. A person with alcohol or drug addiction can receive help and acceptance in the community—even a pat on the back. But those with an addiction of this sort are labeled outcasts and untouchables, objects of hatred and aggression—not only us, but those who support us.

I put my trust in my fellow man only to be rejected; but

I thank God that He has not rejected me. Rather, He offers me a welcome home much like the story of the prodigal son who returned home, probably still smelling of the swine he had been feeding and eating with.

This letter doesn't come easy but with tears and fear as I reach out for help once more, much like a beggar who reaches, not out of desire, but out of necessity.

In asking for help, I also ask for help for my wife and children who are victims also. My wife, who was sexually abused as a child, has to live with the feelings and emotions of her abuse all over again. She desperately needs encouragement in the Lord and guidance, spiritually and emotionally.

Feel free to use the contents of this letter, withholding the name of my wife and our last name. I hope this reaches others who feel no hope, who are looking for understanding and encouragement. For the only place one can find peace is in a personal commitment and relationship with our God and Creator.

There are few more effective ways to debase a life and destroy a reputation than sexual addiction. There are few sins harder to break away from. But through the power of God, it is possible.

Are you trapped in the quagmire of pornography? Do you have magazines you hope your parents or your wife don't know about?

Do you and your husband watch so-called adult videos together after the kids are in bed?

When your work takes you away from home overnight, are you indulging in entertainment at night spots or in your hotel room that you wouldn't want your friends to know about?

If you are involved in pornography, you already know what you are doing is wrong. You may deny its hold on you. But there is good news. You can be clean again. God is waiting to give you back your lost purity. But you need to act immediately, before you are enticed any deeper into the black vortex of corrosive sensuality. We'll explain how in the next chapter.

9

Pursuing Purity

Suppose, like Aladdin, you were given a magic lamp, with one free wish, and only one. If you could have anything you wanted—anything at all—what would it be?

Here's what I would choose: I would ask to see the face of God. I long to behold the most beautiful face in the universe; not just once, but forever. Compared to this, all else pales into insignificance.

You don't need a magic lamp; you need a pure heart. Jesus said that the pure in heart would see God (Matthew 5:8). What an incredible destiny! That's too fabulous a prospect to give up for momentary titillation. When a person saturates the mind with immoral sounds and images, it is impossible to maintain purity of heart before God. We have to choose between these things or preparing ourselves for the ultimate ecstasy: seeing God.

Perhaps that is why Jesus spoke so strongly when He said:

> If your eye causes you to sin, pluck it out and throw it away. It is better for you to enter life with one eye than to have two eyes and be thrown into the fire of hell (Mark 9:47).

In other words, we must root out of our lives anything that tempts us to moral impurity, no matter what the cost. Our rejection of sin must be radical and complete. Paul explained what this entails:

> But among you there must not be even a hint of sexual immorality, or of any kind of impurity, or of greed, because these are improper for God's holy people. Nor should there be obscenity, foolish talk or coarse joking, which are out of place, but rather thanksgiving. For of this you can be sure: No immoral, impure or greedy person . . . has any inheritance in the kingdom of God. . . . Let no one deceive you with empty words, for because of such things God's wrath comes on those who are disobedient. Therefore do not be partners with them (Ephesians 5:3-7).

Anything which encourages my imagination to play with immorality is out of bounds, such as R-rated and most PG-13-rated videos, filthy music, and most soap operas and cheap romance novels. These things are just not worth the loss of integrity or the break in communion with God.

Bombarded daily as we are with impurity, we are tempted to capitulate. We don't approve, but we throw up our hands, saying, "What can we do about it?"

We can refuse to surrender. We can strain the media through the sieve of Philippians 4:8, and watch only whatever is true, noble, right, pure, lovely, admirable, excellent, and praiseworthy.

Christian organizations have had some success in ridding communities of sexually oriented businesses. Anti-porn campaigns have been somewhat effective in recent years. Boycotts and other measures have reduced the availability of pornography in many towns and cities. Some crude sexual programming has even been forced off some satellite television outlets. The United States Justice Department has actively pursued child pornographers.

But legislative action and vigorous enforcement of obscenity statutes, as important as these things are, will not make a society pure. Christians cannot, like salt, preserve society from corruption if they themselves are slowly capitulating to ever lower standards of decency and nobility in books, films, video, and television.

Most Americans belong to a church. More than half

claim to be born again. Sadly, the viewing habits of many North American churchgoers are hardly different from those of their neighbors. If all Christians refused to buy anything, read anything, or watch anything that celebrated illicit sex, the market would drastically shrink.

How do you become pure in heart? Ask God's forgiveness, make Him Lord of your life, and ask Him for the gift of self-control. The way to get rid of sinful habits is to follow the advice of Colossians 3:5, 6:

> Put to death, therefore, whatever belongs to your earthly nature: sexual immorality, impurity, lust, evil desires, and greed, which is idolatry. Because of these, the wrath of God is coming.

How do you put something to death? By starving it. Our sexual natures will always be with us, but by starving them of illicit stimulation and by calling on the power of God through prayer, we can bring them into submission.

Christ said that it was "out of the heart" that "proceed evil thoughts, murders, adulteries," and so forth. Individual acts of sin are external symptoms of a deeper disease that festers within.

So we cannot afford to feed the disease. There is a fire within you; never bring any gasoline anywhere near it, because if you do, there will be a firestorm. Whenever you read certain kinds of novels or watch certain programs or movies, you are feeding the sinful nature. Don't add more fuel to the flame. In the seductive society we live in, the eyes must be controlled. When David's roving eye fell upon bathing Bathsheba one day, it messed up his entire life. A sadder but wiser David wrote in Psalm 101:3, "I will set no wicked thing before my eyes."

Job 31:1 says, "I have made a covenant with my eyes; how then could I gaze upon a virgin?"

Paul says in Romans 16:19, "I want you to be wise about what is good, and innocent about what is evil." 1 Corinthians 14:20 says "In regard to evil be infants."

Let's get down to the nitty-gritty. If a show comes on television that contradicts your Christian values, change the channel. Or find a good book to read. Make a phone call, or write a letter, or take a walk. Or turn out the light and go to bed early for a change so you can get a head start on tomorrow with a clear conscience.

If I find myself unable to stay away from programs my conscience condemns, what can I do?

I can cancel my cable subscription. There are many normal, happy, productive people in North America who have chosen not to pay for cable service. Instead of paying for a service that is corrupting me, I could donate the money to my local church or to the Voice of Prophecy for the spread of the gospel.

I can sell or discard my television set. Some healthy families actually choose not to own one. They cannot imagine finding the time to spend in front of it. They're not missing much. Television today is a wasteland.

Some people think it's important to watch movies and television in order to understand the real world. But that's not the real world. If you want to get in touch with the real world of human hurt, volunteer to work at a county mental health facility or a crisis pregnancy center. There you will encounter enough immorality and foul language to last you a lifetime. And you will see it in the proper context—as tragic behavior on the part of broken people instead of glamorous behavior on the part of a screen hero.

Of course, you must discard and destroy any pornography you possess. When the citizens of Ephesus heard the gospel and repented, they burned over a million dollars worth of evil books in a public bonfire (Acts 19:19).

When you remove the evil from your life, it leaves a void that must be filled with something good. So use the replacement principle. If you have a problem with lust, don't think about the problem; think about something positive and uplifting. Generally, we can only think of one thing at a time. Find something to divert your attention—a worthwhile book or cassette. Replace your television time with a new project or hobby.

It is critically important to set aside time to fill your mind with the Word of God. David wrote in Psalm 119:11, "Thy Word have I hid in my heart that I might not sin against thee." Ask the Holy Spirit to teach you how to apply that Word to every area of your life. Allow nothing to enter the portals of the mind except that which is true, noble, right, pure, lovely, and admirable. As you do so, the God of peace will be with you and keep you pure.

Finally, one of the ways God makes His power available to us is described in James 5:16: "Confess your sins to each other and pray for each other so that you may be healed." Some types of healing require mutual confession.

We do not need to confess to an earthly priest. God hears our prayer. But the only way that many who are snared in pornography can receive God's liberating power is to humble themselves and admit to another believer the whole shameful story. If you are a pastor (and as I write, two letters from pastors with this addiction are sitting on my desk), you may need to find someone outside your congregation to help you. Perhaps a fellow pastor you can trust, perhaps a Christian counselor. You need someone to pray with you and hold you accountable until you are free of this addiction.

If you do not know anyone you can trust, write us at the Voice of Prophecy. We can put you in touch with trained Christian professionals who can counsel you and pray with you by telephone. Of course, we will maintain absolute confidentiality.

Whatever it takes, friend, break free. Your family will benefit. You will be a free person again. And God and all the angels of heaven will rejoice that you have come home.

10

The Tyranny of Self

A religious teacher once asked Jesus, "Of all the commandments, which is the most important?" Jesus replied by quoting two passages from the writings of Moses:

> The most important one . . . is this: 'Hear, O Israel, the Lord our God, the Lord is one. Love the Lord your God with all your heart and with all your soul and with all your mind and with all your strength.' The second is this; 'Love your neighbor as yourself.' There is no commandment greater than these (Mark 12:28-31).

The supreme objective of life is to love God with our entire being; the second major purpose of life is to love others with at least as much care and energy as we expend on ourselves. Simply put, human beings were designed to love and to be loved. That's what life is all about.

"Wait a minute!" you say. "Isn't the elevation of love as the great ideal the very notion that led to the sexual revolution in the first place and gave us so much disease and death?"

No. It was not the elevation but the distortion of love that spawned the sexual revolution. Love, as Jesus taught it, is not a sentiment, a warm feeling, or a glandular urge. Love is a resolute, courageous decision to make the well-being of another more important than one's own well-being.

This love is illustrated by God's reaction to human

sinfulness, which estranged us from God and from life itself. God so loved the world, that he gave his Son to die in order that humans might live (John 3:16). It was not pleasant for God the Father to send His Son into a hostile world; it was not pleasant for the Son to come. God could have solved the problem of sin by abandoning or obliterating sinners. This would have saved Him endless trouble. But God loved us so much that He resolved to sacrifice Himself to save us.

On the night before He was crucified, Jesus told His disciples, "Greater love has no one than this, that one lay down his life for his friends. . . . Love each other," He challenged them, "as I have loved you" (John 15:12, 13).

Love means reaching out to bless others. It is far more than just looking for someone who is pleasant to be with, or finding Mr. Right or my Dream Girl. These things are the stuff of romance. That kind of light-headed, giddy love is a chemical in the brain, which, unfortunately, does not last.

On the other hand, biblical love—the love which Jesus was talking about when He commanded us to love one another—is a tough resolve to bless someone else.

Our society tends to substitute various forms of self-concern for love. More and more, the supreme objective in life is not love or service to others, but self-actualization. "Finding one's self" or "loving myself" is seen as the first and most important business of life. Love for others is okay, people say, if you have taken care of yourself first.

Many men will make any sacrifice to advance their career. Marriage, relationships with their children, connection with God—anything is expendable in the pursuit of more money, prestige, or power.

More and more men and women are choosing to ignore their parents, because when they were young, their parents failed them in some way. Or because spending time with Mom and Dad is not enjoyable and caring for them is costly and difficult. Since they do not seem to derive personal benefit from the relationship, they justify their neglect.

The idealization of self-centered living is presented in art, literature, movies, philosophy. Some artists argue that they have no responsibility to the viewer. Their sole accountability is to themselves. They insist on the freedom to express any impulse they sense within themselves without any self-restraint or concern for those who will see their work. Novels and movies portray ever sicker individuals engaging in unspeakable wickedness, and the reader or viewer is expected to find some sympathy for these individuals without passing judgment on them.

We could dismiss amoral movies and novels and profane and nonsense art if it were not for the fact that we see the same pattern of thinking invading the Christian church. Much of Christianity is self-absorbed. Christians are much more concerned with getting saved than with serving and honoring Christ.

There are even preachers who encourage Christians to believe that doing God's will never includes real sacrifice. Having a comfortable house, driving an expensive car, and dressing well have equal claim on our resources with feeding the starving multitudes of the world or bringing the gospel to those in darkness. Some spend huge sums to have nice church facilities. Then, after the thick carpet and pipe organ and sound system and padded pews are paid for, the leftovers can go to spread the gospel in foreign lands.

Even in discussions of motherhood we can see a change of priorities in our society. A baby is spoken of as just another competitor for a mother's time and energy. Children are seen as a threat to a woman's self-development. In the United States, the vast majority of abortions are not done to save a mother's life or to rescue a girl from the consequences of incest or rape. They are performed because having a baby would be "inconvenient."

Most divorces do not result from violence or adultery. Rather, when one or both spouses decide they are not being fulfilled in the marriage, they divorce to free themselves for a more self-satisfying relationship. Unfortunately, they take their problems with them. The new relationship usually begins to develop the same problems as the old one.

Some people will argue that love and affection are what really make a marriage; and once that love and affection are gone, they aren't really married any more. So they look outside their marriage for that which is lacking within it.

But clinical studies of people involved in adultery clearly demonstrate that adultery does not increase one's happiness. Instead it increases one's personal misery.

Besides, it is a mistake to assume that when the first thrills of marriage lessen, love has died.

For a three-year-old, the first trip to the swimming pool can be very exciting—all the noise, the splashing, the paddling. But as he gets older, the excitement of dog-paddling fades. Yet he doesn't get out of the pool and decide never to go back. He learns to swim. Then to dive.

Love is like that, too. At first, it's all romance. Everything is roses and candlelight. The feelings are intense, full of wonder, excitement, and mystery. Eventually the excitement fades a little. But that doesn't mean that love has ended! It only means that love is changing, growing, expanding to include other pleasures—like security, trust, companionship, and growth. The longer it continues, the deeper and steadier it becomes.

So if you've lost the heart-stopping excitement of your first week of marriage, don't decide that you've fallen out of love. Don't go looking for a new partner, either. Ignore your feelings and keep on doing loving things. Since we can change our feelings by changing our actions, loving actions will ultimately produce loving feelings. You're making a long-term investment in an exclusive relationship, which offers long-term enjoyment.

Listen, friend, once you've made a commitment to love someone until death breaks the bond, stay with it! Even when your mate doesn't deserve it, keep on loving—just as

God keeps on loving you when you don't deserve it. More often than not, that love will be returned to you, many times over.

The teachings of Jesus flatly contradict the ideal of a self-centered life. He calls us to love *regardless*; He teaches us to love *although*. Sometimes that kind of love is hard work. It's certainly not always golden sunsets and warm breezes. It's not always the emotionally stimulating, pleasurable sensations of romance. Caring for a sick baby or a failing parent can be challenging, taxing work. But this kind of caring is real love, and it contains the seeds of enduring joy.

In fact, the ultimate goal of sexual love is not pleasure, but a lengthy process which at times might be considered rather unpleasant. While sex is not *just* for reproduction, yet procreation might be considered its ultimate purpose. That love-making can actually create life is its crowning wonder and glory. The miracle of childbirth reminds us that the goal of love is caring for those who cannot care for themselves. Having a child is a thrill that calls us to the highest ideals of service and love.

Jesus calls us to love sacrificially. He summons us to bear a cross, to struggle against sin and darkness. It is the struggle of bearing the cross that leads to genuine happiness. In John 10:10, Jesus said, "I have come that you might have life and have it in all its fullness." He wasn't exaggerating.

Every barrier God places on our natural impulses is really a stair step toward total freedom. When we make biblical love the controlling rule of our life, we are protected against the lies of the sexual revolution; and the way is opened for us to experience the rich, untainted satisfaction of a life dedicated to loving others.

11

Out of the Scrap Heap

If you've read this far, I admire your motivation. Perhaps you have found some of this material discouraging. Perhaps you, like most people, have fallen short of complete lifelong purity. This chapter is for you. It's about God's amazing, restoring grace.

One of my friends moved to Times Square in New York City right after grad school. Since this was his first job, he could not afford to spend much money on furniture. So he mastered the art of scavenging. He furnished nearly his entire apartment with stuff he found discarded on the street.

Even today, twelve years later, his home office is full of second-hand treasures. His desk, chair, and printer stand, several of his book cases, the table that holds his plant collection, and the largest plants in his collection all came from the streets. He learned to see treasure where others only saw trash.

God is also a master at recycling garbage. He sees priceless treasures for His kingdom where others see only broken, wasted lives.

Before Jesus came to earth as a human baby, He lived in heaven as God. Unlike you and me, He was able to choose His own ancestors.

When we read His genealogy in Matthew 1, we discover that all down the line from Abraham, the father of the Hebrews, to Jesus the Messiah, the bloodline does not pass automatically from firstborn to firstborn. King David, for example, was, in fact, the youngest of eight brothers. But God chose him as the ancestor of Jesus Christ. In each generation God the Son made a specific choice of the mother and father He wanted included in His bloodline.

One of the biggest surprises in Matthew's record of Jesus' ancestors is his mention of four women. In those days women were not named in genealogies. The fact that these women are included alerts us to look for some special meaning in their stories. Let's consider the first in the list, Tamar.

Tamar was a Canaanite who married the oldest son of a man named Judah. Her story is told in Genesis 38. Her husband died before they had any children, so following the practice of the time, her late husband's next-younger brother, Onan, married her to provide her with children. Onan used Tamar sexually, but he deliberately avoided getting her pregnant. Because of Onan's callous exploitation of his wife, God caused him to die.

Tamar's father-in-law, Judah, then promised that she could marry the youngest brother when he was old enough. Tamar went home to live with her parents. Years passed. The youngest son of Judah reached marriageable age, and nothing happened. Tamar began to doubt that Judah would ever keep his promise that she would marry his last son. And she was desperate for a child.

Finally she hit on a rather devious plan. Judah's wife had died, and Tamar learned that he was going to travel to a distant town to visit a friend. Carefully disguising herself, she dressed as a prostitute, then stationed herself at a strategic spot along the road that Judah would take to his friend's house. She figured Judah's loneliness and his sexual needs would overcome his scruples once he got away from home and people who knew him.

Sure enough, she was right. Judah fell for her plot. He did not see past her disguise, even when he slept with her.

Several months later, Judah found out his daughter-in-law was pregnant, and no one knew who the father was. He was outraged. She had shamed the good name of the whole family. He demanded she be put to death for prostitution. As she was being led out to her execution, she stopped the procession and produced proof that Judah was the father. Confronted with the evidence, he confessed his responsibility. "She is more righteous than I," he admitted.

Now if you were God, what would you do with these two? A hypocritical, lying man. An abused, desperate woman. Would you write them off as hopeless reprobates? As moral garbage? Would you look the other way and pretend it didn't happen?

What did God do? God bypassed Judah's three older brothers and chose him as an ancestor of the Messiah. God chose Tamar, a member of the pagan Canaanites, a woman who got herself pregnant by her father-in-law, to become an ancestor of Jesus.

Another woman mentioned in Jesus' geneology is Rahab the prostitute (Matthew 1:5). She is mentioned two other times in the New Testament as an example of a woman of faith (Hebrews 11:31, James 2:35). Jesus took a prostitute and chose her as His ancestor, giving her an honorable future.

Another notable ancestor of Jesus was David, who had an affair with Bathsheba. Yet Jesus was called "The Son of David."

It is impossible for human beings to make such a wreck of their lives that God can do nothing with them. Human mistakes and helplessness cannot overwhelm the creative power of God. He can save from the uttermost to the guttermost.

Have you made a mess of your life? Have you allowed loneliness or desperation to overcome your self-control?

Does it seem to you that because of your mistakes, there is nothing God can do with you? Don't you believe it! The Creator of the Universe is larger than all your sins, larger than all your weaknesses and failures. And He has a place for you on His team.

Jesus' genealogy reveals that even before He appeared on earth as a baby, He cared for broken people. He has always been a friend of sinners. He has always loved the unacceptable. He has always seen treasure where everyone else saw only garbage. And He works the same way today. Here is God's promise to those who have been unfaithful to Him:

> "For I know the plans I have for you," declares the LORD, "plans to prosper you and not to harm you, plans to give you hope and a future. Then you will call upon me and come and pray to me, and I will listen to you. You will seek me and find me when you seek me with all your heart" (Jeremiah 29:11-14).

God has a good future planned for you, no matter what lies in your past. Divorce, abuse, dishonesty, alcohol and other drugs—yes, even incest—none of these things makes God helpless. God will pick through the garbage of your life and find something He can cultivate and transform into a masterpiece that honors Him. He is eager to give you a hope and a future. He will "repay you for the years the locust have eaten" (Joel 2:25). His grace is truly amazing.

> "Come now, let us reason together," says the LORD. "Though your sins are like scarlet, they shall be as white as snow; though they are red as crimson, they shall be like wool" (Isaiah 1:18).

If you are sifting the cinders of a burnt-out existence without joy or hope, then let me tell you that out of ashes can come beauty.

Ashes are mostly carbon, which is the basic building block of life. All living matter has a chemistry that is based upon the element carbon in various combinations with other elements. So one might say that ashes are the basis of life.

Now, if you had a machine that was powerful enough, you could gather up carbon ashes from your fireplace and place those ashes inside that machine, apply tremendous pressure and heat, and make a diamond. A diamond is only carbon—only rearranged ashes. That's something God can do with ashes. God likes to make diamonds out of ashes.

Do you have any ashes? What about the ashes of addiction? Of resentment? Of immorality? Of failure? Of rejection? Of abuse? The ashes of a broken relationship?

God can give beauty for ashes.

The citizens hardly noticed the small, lone plane flying overhead toward the heart of the city. They were used to waves of allied bombers that came to drop their deadly loads. One plane didn't mean much. A small package was seen to fall from the plane as it turned and flew away. A blinding flash, and the holocaust engulfed and destroyed Hiroshima, leaving ashes instead of beauty. A nation was brought to its knees and surrendered.

And then a strange thing happened. Out of the ashes of the tiny nation of Japan was built over the next forty years the most modern, most efficient, most highly industrialized economy in the world. Tiny Japan, about the size of the state of Montana, became an economic giant, threatening even the mighty United States of America. Out of weakness came strength. Out of ashes came beauty.

God can do the same for you when, like Japan, you surrender.

Jesus is in the recycling business. He picks wasted men and women up out of the junk heap of human depravity and restores their honor, and recycles them into display pieces in His museum, where they are a spectacle to men and angels.

One of the worst junk heaps of human depravity in ancient times was the seaport of Corinth. Just about every kind of wickedness that can be found in Los Angeles or New York today could be found in Corinth. But God raised up a Christian congregation of recycled sinners in Corinth. In 1 Corinthians 6:9-11 Paul writes about some of those church members whose lives had been transformed by the gospel:

> Do you not know that the wicked will not inherit the kingdom of God? Do not be deceived: Neither the sexually immoral nor idolaters nor adulterers nor male prostitutes nor homosexual offenders nor thieves nor the greedy nor drunkards nor slanderers nor swindlers will inherit the kingdom of God. *And that is what some of you were.* But you were washed, you were sanctified, you were justified in the name of the Lord Jesus Christ and by the Spirit of our God.

In 2 Corinthians, Paul says that we are temples for God's presence. The Lord actually wants to dwell with us. "I will dwell in them and walk among them; and I will be their God and they shall be My people" (2 Corinthians 2:16). Then Paul says,

> Since we have these promises, dear friends, let us purify ourselves from everything that contaminates body and spirit, perfecting holiness out of reverence for God (2 Corinthians 7:1).

So what should you do? If you have lost your purity, then kneel down now and surrender everything to Him—your sins, your failures, your shame, your ambitions, your possessions, your all. Ask God to restore you to purity, to give you an honorable future. If you are single and have lost your virginity, ask God to heal the wounds and give you a brand-new virginity. If you, like many sexually active teenagers, are searching for the love that you never received from your parents, ask God to provide it.

Then decide just how far on the ladder of intimacy (see page 37) you want to go with your relationships.

Next, sit down and do some serious thinking about what you are going to say when someone asks you to go too far. Perhaps something like this: "I respect you more than that." Or "I couldn't do that to myself (or my parents, or my future spouse)." Think up several strong answers that will not offend, and make them part of your repertoire.

The final step is extremely important. If you are single, sit down and write a letter to your future mate. Do this whether you have sexual sins in your past or not. In that letter, explain to your future mate why you are choosing to keep yourself pure for him or her, so that you can give him or her all of yourself on your wedding night. Talk about your future children. Express your highest ideals.

When you are finished, seal the letter, stamp it, and mail a copy to yourself (to give it an authentic postmarked date). Place it *unopened* in a safe place. Keep it until you meet the one you want to spend your life with, then give it to that person after you become engaged.

One more thing. If you want to make my day, write me at The Voice of Prophecy, Box 55, Los Angeles, 90053, and tell me about your decision.

May God bless you and keep you, and make His face to shine upon you, and give you peace.

The Family First

The Family First

Kenneth O. Gangel

HIS INTERNATIONAL SERVICE
Minneapolis, MN 55423 U.S.A.

Printed in the U.S.A.

Published by His International Service
Minneapolis, Minn. 55423 U.S.A.

Standard Book Number 911802-28-2

Library of Congress Catalog
Card Number 72-75944

What Makes A Young Rebel? Fall, 1970
Pop Rock And Christian Teens Fall, 1969
Give Me Guidelines To Live By Fall, 1968
© *Today's Living* Baptist Publications
The above articles have been adapted for use in chapters VI,
VII and VIII, respectively, and are used by permission of the
publishers.

Scripture quotations are reprinted by permission from the fol-
lowing publishers:
From *THE AMPLIFIED BIBLE*, Old Testament © Copyright 1962,
64 Zondervan Publishing House, Grand Rapids, Michigan.
From *THE AMPLIFIED BIBLE AND NEW TESTAMENT* © Copy-
right 1958 The Lockman Foundation, La Habra, California.
From *THE LIVING BIBLE* © Copyright 1971 Tyndale House
Publishers, Wheaton, Illinois.
From *THE NEW ENGLISH BIBLE* © Copyright The Delegates
of the Oxford University Press and the Syndics of the Cambridge
University Press 1961, 1970.
From *THE NEW TESTAMENT IN THE LANGUAGE OF THE
PEOPLE*, by Charles B. Williams © Copyright 1966 Edith S. Wil-
liams. Published by Moody Press, Moody Bible Intitute of Chi-
cago, Illinois.

Foreword

This book is a straightforward honest attempt to meet head on a major problem in contemporary society and in our evangelical churches. Unfortunately the contemporary pulpit and Christian educators all too frequently will decry the evil of our day and exhort their flocks to eschew sexual immorality, and to uphold the purity and integrity of the family, but they are lamentably on the short end of solid constructive help. As Dr. Gangel writes: "One of the problems we face in this (family) relationship in the twentieth century is a hesitancy on the part of church leaders to tackle the really difficult problems of family life. Most pastors, for example, are quite happy to stay away from subjects like premarital sex, early marriages and divorce. One pastor of a reasonably large church told me just a short time ago that he never mentions his views on divorce publicly. If people want to hear what he has to say, he will talk about it in the privacy of his study."

This is applying bandaids where major surgery is needed. What our evangelical churches need is a frank facing up to the problems that confront the church and a long term, carefully planned program of Biblical preaching and Biblical instruction. In this volume, *"The Family First,"* Dr. Kenneth Gangel seeks to provide for the pastor, the church worker, the Sunday

School teacher, and the Christian parent some clear line of guidance as to the necessity of such "family education" and as to its content if it is to be informed by the teaching of Holy Scripture.

The volume is written in lively readable fashion, avoids the smack of prudery so often discernible in discussions stemming from those of Puritan background, but also written in good taste—a virtue sometimes neglected by those who are too fearful of appearing prudish. Above all, Dr. Gangel is unapologetically Bibilcal as he seeks to lead his readers to grapple boldly and faithfully with the gritty problems facing all evangelical churches today. Once again he proves for us that to be radically **Biblical** is also to be radically **relevant** in today's world.

For the sake of his readers who are not acquainted with the author of this volume, I should like to conclude this foreword with a personal note. *The Family First* is not the product of an armchair theorist. This volume has grown out of a busy career of teaching and counseling several generations of students. More important still it flows from the life of a man of God who has put his theory into practice within the intimacy of his own family circle.

Kenneth S. Kantzer
Dean, Trinity Evangelical Divinity School

Prologue

The Family First. Does the title appear a bit dogmatic? Perhaps. But from Eden to Eternity; from the creation of the first Adam to the reign of the last Adam; from Deuteronomy 6 to Ephesians 6, God makes it clear that the primary social and instructional group in all the world is the family.

And there is no reason to believe that His plan has changed. God doesn't play by our rules or march to the beat of earthly drummers. His truth is absolute. Secular sociologists may reject the family but the Heavenly Father still expects earthly fathers to pattern their homes after His Biblical blueprint.

This little handbook was born in many classroom sessions in a Christian college. It was fed and nourished by hundreds of people in Family Life Education conferences all across the country. The intended purpose is service as a manual for Sunday school classes and training hour groups as well as general reading by parents and prospective parents.

May the God of love fill the hearts of all who read, so that their homes may reflect the beauty and glow of His perfect love.

KOG
Deerfield, Ill.

March, 1972

*To my nieces and nephews
— all ten of them —
soon to face these
crucial years and issues*

Contents

1

The Family Today

The family is in trouble. Having once occupied a place of primary importance in society, the home has now been relegated by many to a position of considerably lesser importance. One writer discusses what he calls "social sicknesses" and points out that such sicknesses may very well be different symptoms of the same disease, namely, cultural disintegration. In his list, Brown includes "family disorganization" in the same category as juvenile delinquency, prostitution, sex offenses, and crime. He goes on to say,

> "The old primary groupings have been broken up—the family, the working group, the village council—and replaced by huge, anonymous bodies in relation to which status, function, and personal significance are lost".[1]

There is little doubt that family life in Western society has been subjected to massive transformation in the twentieth century. Some scholars view this as legitimate change to meet the evolving context of society. Others, like Brown, talk about "disintegration" of family life. Radical psychologists like Harold Feldman of New York State College at Cornell even advocate state control over parenthood. Feldman takes the position that

---

1. J. A. C. Brown, *The Social Psychology of Industry*, Baltimore: Penguin Books, 1954, p. 270.

11

parental competency should be decided by social scientists. He suggests that scientists attempt to train couples who do not meet their standards for parenthood and, until certain tests are passed, they would not be permitted to have children. Upon being asked how society would regulate or prevent procreation, Feldman replied that science would soon be able to give medicine at birth that would prevent human fertility until another pill is given when the individual meets the standards for parenthood. Other Feldmanian ideas include a recognition of the unnecessary character of marriage, an emphasis on easy divorce, and the possibility of "group marriages."

One of the most significant aspects of the problem sociologically is that disintegration of family life might very well be a source of other problems which disturb Western culture. In this democratic society the home has historically been considered as the central agency of control. Educational organizations such as the P.T.A. have consistently attempted to wed other social institutions to the home. Some historians (both secular and Christian) have argued that the breakdown of the home was a problem in the corruption of Ancient Rome and have written rather convincing parallels between the history of that society and the dissolution of family units in our own.

In this kind of context the Christian parent holds no less of a responsibility to raise his children "in the nurture and admonition of the Lord". As a matter of fact, the close parallel between first century and twentieth century culture makes the impact of New Testament admonitions even more poignant and, just as the professional athlete plays a better game when he is familiar with the stadium, so Christian parents today need to recognize the pressures and problems which contemporary society holds for the satisfactory implementation of the Biblical principles of Christian family living. In this first chapter we will briefly consider ten of the more pressing problems which we face.

Urbanization

In the decade of the fifties the rural population in the United States declined for the first time in national history. Describing the mass movement to the cities, *Look* magazine suggests that "As we continue to turn our farms into efficiently mechanized food factories, the end of the trend is nowhere in sight. Everybody is going to town".[2] Sociologist Harvey Wish sees the problem beginning even earlier. In *Society and Thought In Modern America* he devotes an entire chapter to what he calls "the urban impact on the home" and points up that as early as 1917 urbanization had gone far in disintegrating the patriarchal family. No doubt there are some values in urbanization but, according to Wish, the values are grossly outweighed by the difficulties which have been brought about by the disintegration of the home life.

This disintegration of the family has been facilitated by urbanization since the rapid living pace in the city tends to dissect family relationships. Family members find their security and relationships in secondary groups. Editors William Genne and Harold Letts suggest in *Christian Families In Today's World* that urbanization affects not only the people who move to the cities, but the entire population. The point is that the "depletion of population and easy transportation have lessened community consciousness and services. Local schools have been replaced by regional schools. Resident clergy have been replaced by clergy covering several towns, often at great distances from each other". They go on to suggest that one of the biggest negative results of urbanization is de-personalization.

> It is one of the paradoxes of our time that urban culture has brought so many people to live so closely together that they are alone and isolated in the midst of multitudes. Wherever city people go, there are crowds—to work, to school, to shop, to the movies, to the beaches,

---

2. *Look*, September 21, 1965, p. 31.

or the lakes, or even to their homes—yet in the crowds there is seldom a person whom they know by name or who knows them by name. Identity and the individual personality are threatened by mass living and the lack of familial roots. Even the tenuous ties acquired in the factory or school or apartment house can be quickly lost by still another move to a "better" apartment, or a new city, or even a new state.[3]

Industrialization

In the post World War II development of gigantic industry, thousands of persons began to be employed in giant plants covering several acres. Real estate costs in major urban areas (particularly in the East and North Midwest) have driven industry South and West in search of less expensive ground and labor. Meanwhile, industrialization has produced affluence in the society, creating additional leisure time and ownership of things deemed unnecessary or even unattainable ten or twenty years ago.

World War II defense plants reached their long, noisy arms into the kitchens of American families to create "Rosie the riveter". While G.I. Joe was off shooting the bullets, his wife, girlfriend, or sister was back home making them. What apparently was not foreseen in those early forties was that the new working status of women was destined not to be a temporary stopgap measure to assist America in the war, but a whole new pattern of life which has now come to ugly fruition in what is loosely called the "Women's Liberation Movement". A cigarette commercial reminds American women, "You've come a long way baby", but it stops short of suggesting which direction. Genne and Letts suggest that "the era when the women voted 'as their husbands told them' is past. There are a few cultural groups remaining where the social status of

3. Genne & Letts, Eds., *Christian Families in Today's World,* Department of Family Life, NCC: N.Y., N.Y., 1961, p. 11

women is inferior. Although their salary rates are not equal to those of men for the same jobs, they are employed in almost every occupation. Indeed, the present rate of industrialization would not have been possible had the emancipation, and thus the employment of women, not occurred".[4]

The Biblical evaluation of this development, however, must take note of the destruction which it has wrought to role delineation. In the desert tent Abraham had no difficulty in maintaining his spiritual and familial leadership over Sarah, but then Sarah never worked in a defense plant or drove her own car. The oft-repeated Biblical injunction to submission and obedience has been relegated to the wastebasket of worthless relics from a former day.

Mobility

Reports from the United States Census Bureau indicate that the average family moves eight times during its existence, and each year one family in every five moves across county lines. Such transiency destroys family roots and makes it difficult for a child to determine where "home" really is or was. Ties with other families must be sufficiently loose to be severed on short notice. Changing relationships in neighborhood, school, church, and the larger community become a pattern of life.

All of this provides at the same time a standardization (living side by side with dozens of other families in a housing development consisting of identical homes) and a dependence upon society's benefits for a sense of security. Genne and Letts show how security and conformity are Siamese twins in society today.

> The modern American family, in spite of its mobility, has more material security than its predecessors. The standardization which threatens its individuality at the same time provides a pattern of living into which it can fall comfortably in each new community. Its

---

4. Ibid.

improved standard of living, while subject to the hazards of economic fluctuations, has a bulwark of publicly sponsored insurance against crippling unemployment and death, as well as both public and industry-sponsored provisions for retirement income. The mass employment of women has led to the prevalence of "two salaried families" where the husband's income is supplemented by a small income from the full-time or part-time work of the wife. The higher level of education is gradually offering the security of steadier employment. The reliance of the American family upon security has become so widespread that there is resultant loss of individual initiative and the will to pioneer.[5]

Divorce and Separation

Many secular sociologists point to divorce as an adaptation to a changing culture rather than an example of deterioration of the family group. Those who are concerned with the Biblical point of view, however, even though they may take differing positions on the acceptability and permissibility of divorce, will surely all agree that widespread divorce and separation is a negative crucial factor in Western family life. In viewing the current scene Scudder suggests that "present conditions clearly establish the fact that the family has in modern times deteriorated both as a social control and as a redemptive and stabilizing fellowship".[6]

Although divorce and separation are certainly not identical, the result is often the same. Statistics on divorce are notoriously deceiving and almost any kind of argument can be made, depending upon what resource is used. Conservative estimates might generalize at approximately one out of three nationally, and one out of two in certain critical areas such as Southern California. One thing is clear. Family instability in Western Society today is a reality, and the situation is

---

5. Ibid., pp. 8,9, 11..
6. C. W. Scudder, *The Family in Christian Perspective,* Nashville: Broadman Press, 1962, p. 8.

worsening rather than improving. When separations and desertions are added to the divorce statistics, the national figure pushes 50% and in some estimates even goes beyond. Elton Trueblood refers to divorce as "an admission of failure in the most sacred undertaking in one's life". An entire chapter will be devoted to this issue later in the book.

Substitute Parents and Fatherless Children

The great tragedy of family breakdown is the result which it has on the lives of the children. Frequently, divorce, separation or desertion will result in children being reared by others. The problem of professional foster care alone, though only a small evidence of the total picture, presents a formidable negation.

> There are only one hundred and thirty thousand adoptions a year: of these, half are by relatives and thus are not even adoptions in the sense in which they arouse so much interest. There are three hundred thousand children in foster care in institutions costing American taxpayers many hundreds of millions of dollars a year. The cost might seem well worthwhile where the result produces well adjusted citizens. Unfortunately, the evidence is strong that foster care makes worse whatever problems the child, as a result of this earlier often poor home environment, has brought to it.[7]

Of course the broken home is primarily a home without a father. In *Fatherless Families* Wynn deplores the fact that "we do not know enough about how to compensate a child for the loss of his father. The consequence of that loss and the effect on the child of being brought up without a father or father substitute have not been sufficiently studied".[8] The problem is self-perpetuating because the broken home becomes a breeding ground for broken homes. This is surely not always the case, but a child with negative familial ex-

---

7. Isaac Rael, *Adopting a Child Today*, p. 148.
8. Wynn, Margaret. *Fatherless Families*. New York: British Book Centre, Inc., 1964.

perience is a candidate for the construction of another deteriorating family situation resting on social, psychological, and often spiritual deficiencies.

Dave Wilkerson writes about Larry, "a product of affluent neglect. By the time he became a parent he was such a miserable excuse for a human being, that he simply could not handle responsibility and therefore was unable to function as either a husband or a father".[9] Sometimes strong maternal leadership can substitute for the absence of the father but more frequently successful child rearing is accomplished in the absence of a father by the introduction into the family picture of a strong paternal image such as a pastor, uncle, or even grandfather.

Low Moral Standards

The elevation of low moral standards in the public media was the subject of an interesting *McCall's* article in 1965 entitled "Let's Face It". The author of the article indicates that the new heroine "of what might loosely be called our culture" is the prostitute.[10]

> Yet—in the prey of the sex-cult themselves, whether they know it or not—the maternal desire to have their girls "popular" and hence marriageable is probably stronger than their disapproval of the means they use to be so.

Obviously to say that moral standards are "low" one has assumed a certain level at which such standards should be set. Speaking sociologically it would be proper to say that "low" moral standards are those which lead people to make light of or attack the sanctity of marriage, the family, and the home. More pointedly, however, moral standards are relatively "low" to the extent that they disagree with the standards and principles of the Word of God.

---

9. David Wilkerson, *Parents on Trial,* New York: Hawthorne Books, 1967, p. 73.

10. "Let's Face It", *McCalls, p.* 18, June 1965.

Pressured Schedules

Western society today lives by the clock. Activities of all kinds headed by the dominating schedule of the public school clamor for the attention of each family member. If there should be a lull in school activities there is always the demand of community groups like the Lion's, Kiwanis, or other civic organizations.

Recreation is also a prime value of our culture. As leisure time increases it appears that the four day week will become a reality for most workers in the 1970s. Little League, bowling teams, and a host of spectator sports offer ample opportunity for people to be away from home.

And the church hasn't helped the situation. Rather than seeking to mold the family back into a functioning unit, the church often schedules programs several **nights in the** week, each drawing the attention of one or two family members and leaving the rest at home. In our harried effort to live by the clock, we have confused programs with productivity, meetings with meaning, and success with spirituality.

Secularization and Materialism

The affluence of the society has a tendency to breed constant demand for more things. The family's "wants" rather than its "needs" dictate the work schedules. No doubt there are a number of families in which the wife is working so that the basic needs can be met. It is just as sure, however, that in many families the motivation for maternal employment is materialistic. John Dewey once applauded the shift in American Society from a dependence upon certainty to a dependence upon security, but it is largely this shift which has created two-salaried families.

The value system of the affluent society has been greatly altered. Once spiritually and morally oriented, it now functions with a largely secularistic point of view, and in the home more is caught than taught regarding value systems. It is generally agreed that parents project on their children their own interests, preferences, prejudices, ambitions, and the like. The child identifies himself rather closely with his parents, and looks upon them as his models long before he identifies himself with people outside the family.

Strained Family Relations

Bill Vaughn's caricature of the American family describes everyone sitting numbly in front of his own television set, eating his own T.V. dinner, and waiting for his own telephone to ring. He suggests that the American family is in danger of becoming "a loose confederation of separate entities or, at best (or worst) a Common Market". Divorce and separation statistics, of course, show only a part of the picture. What is referred to in a later chapter as "practical divorce" points up that a husband and wife living legally under one roof may, for all practical purposes, just as well be living in separate cities.

In a *Moody Manna* devotional book, Dr. Gene Getz cites the research of Appel and Goldberg carried out in the Department of Psychiatry at the University of Pennsylvania. These physicians conclude that the family is "fragmented"; that its members do not hold together as a unit any longer than circumstances compel them to. Divorce is often "postponed for the sake of the children" so that it is not uncommon to see the breakup of marriages twenty years old. In his classic text *Helping Families Through the Church,* Oscar Feucht discusses the necessary emotional maturity incumbent upon adult family members.

> Good emotional control shows itself in such matters as meeting problems instead of evading them, ability to look at both sides of a problem, patience in dealing with another person, avoiding sudden outbursts of anger, starting and closing each day with pleasant conversation, focusing on a problem rather than on the

mistakes of your mate, keeping tensions from building up.[11]

Sociological Detraction

There are those who argue that the family as a unit is not basically important. Some secular sociologists suggest that responsibilities and roles carried out by the family in earlier days of society are now being handled by **larger** social groups, or at least **different** social groups. The family has developed a role of specialization which does not necessarily in any way demonstrate deterioration of its total function.

Such is the picture of the American family in contemporary Western society. More specifically, such is the context in which Christian adults are asked to construct Biblical family units which represent an earthly picture of the relationship between Christ and the church. There is no question about the Biblical position on the primacy of the family. Long before God called into existence schools and churches, He designed the basic unit of society in the garden of Eden. There There is no evidence in Scripture that this emphasis has ever changed. Parental right is a natural right which is neither bestowed nor legalized by the state. It is the purpose of this book to examine Biblical principles and methodology for establishing a Christian home in the kind of alien environment described in the paragraphs of this first chapter.

11. Oscar Feucht, editor, *Helping Families Through the Church*, St. Louis: Concordia Publishing House, 1957, p. 195.

2

What Makes a Home Christian?

The setting painted in chapter one presents a rather grim backdrop for the acting out of Christian family roles. Yet the imperatives of God's Word regarding the importance and primacy of Christian family living are not minimized just because the sociological surroundings are more difficult. Furthermore, the Christian dare not let the secular sociologist determine his view of marriage. A Christian philosophy of marriage and family living can only be properly delineated from the pages of God's Word and fitted in as an important piece in the theological jigsaw puzzle of evangelical Christianity. There is no question that the Christian family is different from the non-Christian family. All of us would give nodding agreement to that conclusion. It is essential, however, if we are going to properly study Christian family living, for us to understand what the distinctives are and how they are ascertained in God's revelation.

A Christian Family Is One Which Properly Understands The Biblical Purposes of Marriage

There are secular purposes for marriage and there are distinctly Christian purposes. In some cases, the two may seem to be very much in agreement. In other cases, there is no possible way to harmonize what God has ordained with man's social meanderings. Not only

22

is it important to clearly identify Christian purposes for marriage, but it is also important to rank those purposes in some understanding of God's priorities. Perhaps the following four items do not compose an exhaustive list on the subject, but they are at least representative of what the Bible has to say regarding why a man should leave his father and mother and attach himself to his wife. And remember, the order is important.

1. Christian Marriage Exists for Fellowship

If this basic principle is not observed, our whole approach to family living may be distorted. In spite of all the wonderful things which God had created in the garden of Eden, Adam was still incomplete. It was insufficient for him to live alone among the animals because not one of them could provide a fitting companion for the man. The words "help meet" in the Authorized Version of Genesis 2:18 and 20 are an unfortunate translation. Even the more modern word "helpmate" does not convey the impact of what God was doing in the garden that day. *The Amplified Bible* captures the dynamic of the passage when it renders verse 18 in the following manner:

> Now the Lord God said, it is not good (sufficient, satisfactory) that the man should be alone; I will make him a helper meet (suitable, adaptable, completing) for him.

If two young people contemplating marriage (or for that matter, a couple who have been married for forty years) do not see the strategic nature of the companionship role as the primary purpose for marriage, they have missed God's plan. All other purposes are secondary. All other factors, as important as they may seem, must take a lower place of esteem in our thinking as Christians. If this cardinal purpose of marriage is not functioning properly, all of the other three purposes will be interior as well.

2. Christian Marriage is for Sexual Fulfillment

There is no record in the early chapters of Genesis

giving us an account of the attitudes or activities of the sexual relationship of Adam and Eve. From other passages of scripture, however, we may assume that their marriage based on spiritual companionship also had physical consummation in the fulfillment of God-given sexual drives. In God's plan, these drives are only to be fulfilled within the marriage bond. The responsibilities of husband and wife to each other in the matter of physical sex are clearly delineated in the seventh chapter of I Corinthians.

> The husband must always give his wife what is due her, and the wife too must do so for her husband. The wife does not have the right to do as she pleases with her own body; the husband has his right to it. In the same way the husband does not have the right to do as he pleases with his own body; the wife has her right to it. You husbands and wives must stop refusing each other what is due, unless you agree to do so just for awhile, so as to have plenty of time for prayer, and then to be together again, so as to keep Satan from tempting you because of your lack of self-control (I Corinthians 7:3-5, *Williams*).

Sometimes in a cursory reading of these verses in the Authorized Version we get the impression that Paul is just speaking about being nice to one another and maintaining an honest and open relationship. The context, however, demands an interpretation that deals with the sexual relationship of husband and wife. A holding back of that part of the marriage responsibility is called "defrauding" and the ground rules are stated in verse five:

A. Abstinence from sexual relationship must be by mutual consent.

B. Abstinence from sexual relationship must be temporary ("for a time").

C. Abstinence from sexual relationship must be for spiritual purposes.

Of course, this is describing a normal situation.

There will be situations of abnormality in which for physical reasons it may be desirable or even necessary to abstain from copulation. In the usual pattern any "defrauding" for inadequate reasons will lead to an openness to temptation by Satan himself. The first part of Hebrews 13:4 also speaks to the issue of this purpose of marriage: "Marriage is honorable in all, and the bed undefiled . . ."

3. Christian Marriage is for Procreation

After Adam and Eve had learned to relate to one another spiritually, emotionally, and physically, they were ready to take responsibility for the development of others. The crowning glory of children in a marriage is a song of praise often sung in the pages of Holy Scripture. In two consecutive Psalms (127 and 128) we read that "Children are an heritage from the Lord; and the fruit of the womb is his reward" and again, "Thy wife shall be as a fruitful vine by the sides of thine house; thy children like olive plants round about thy table". The command to "be fruitful and multiply" was given to Adam and Eve and again to Noah's family when they emerged from the ark.

Perhaps it is important for us to remember in these days of population control that both of these commands were given to families which contained the only human beings on earth at the time that they heard these words of Jehovah. Whatever we may accept as valid among the arguments of planned parenthood and population control, there is no reason that any of them should detract from the fact that the continuation of the race through procreation is one of God's purposes in marriage.

The miracle of creation continues to be a mystery unknown even to the finest scientists of the enlightened twentieth century. David once wrote, "I will praise thee . . . for I am fearfully and wonderfully made" (Psalm 139:14). That testimony is surely echoed by every parent who stands by a crib looking down into the face of a newborn child. Man is the crowning glory of God's creation and the continuation of the process through the biological reproduction of cells is brought about by man's fertilization of the woman's egg. It seems to be such a common and natural process that we often do not recognize the hand of the Divine Creator at work in His world.

Surely one of the reasons for God's design of bringing children into families rather than into school systems or church congregations is commitment to the educational functions of the home. By the process of reproduction parents are not only to continue the race and populate the earth, but also to identify their singular responsibility to nurture that child in the process of growth and development until he becomes an adult and begins the cycle all over again.

4. Christian Marriage is a Lesson in Church Truth

One of the key passages in the New Testament defining the relationship of husbands and wives is Ephesians 5. In this chapter Paul continually draws a comparison between that relationship and the relationship of Christ to the church. The analogy can be approached in two different ways. On one side of the coin, we understand that a Christian husband looks at the example of Christ's love for the church to learn how he is to love his wife. If we turn the coin over, however, we can also infer that the world may learn something about the relationship that Jesus Christ sustains to the church by seeing how a Christian husband loves and sacrifices for his wife. If he nourishes and cherishes his family, his unsaved neighbors may learn something about the way the Lord nourishes and cherishes the church. Without ever having been inside a church building; ever having heard a sermon; or ever reading a page of the Bible; people may learn something about God's truth by observing the behavior of a Christian family!

A Christian Marriage Recognizes
The Biblical Patterns Of Its Existence

What constitutes marriage in God's sight? Are any two people who ever have sexual intercourse married?

Some have so interpreted I Corinthians 6:16 in which Paul warns against associations with prostitutes because "he who is joined to an harlot is one body". However, the passage, while saying that two who are joined together in physical union are one flesh, does not say that all who are of one flesh in this manner are properly married in God's sight. This passage has frequently been used by some well-meaning parents to frighten their young people away from premarital sex. It is no doubt true that Christian young people should not engage in premarital sex, but this is a poor passage for support of that standard.

There is another view sometimes called the "transearthly" or "metaphysical" view of marriage. Persons holding this position simply argue that marriage is purely a heavenly device and no earthly laws or standards can be applied. Consequently, any adherence to earthly legal formats or church wedding procedures is totally irrelevant. If people wish to join their spirits in heavenly marriage, they may do it any time. It should be obvious that such a view is not only a perversion of Romans 13 (submission to legal powers on earth) but also a soft road to license and self-gratification.

The Biblical view and definition of marriage seems to have at least four aspects:

1. Voluntary Agreement

Just as the bride of Christ makes a volitional choice to identify with Him, so Christian marriage properly conceived, is a voluntary agreement on the part of two people to join their lives together. Amos asks the question, "Can two walk together except they be agreed?" (Amos 3:3). The entire tone of scripture leads us to believe that God intends an independent willingness to characterize this crucial decision. The selling of young women into bridal slavery is characteristic of dark paganism, not of Christian truth. The consistent implication in I Corinthians 7 is that the wife and husband have had ample opportunity to decide whether this relationship should be theirs or not.

2. Legal Formulization

The Romans 13 passage mentioned above indicates that Christians are always supposed to be in subjection to the legal structures of the society in which they live. The only New Testament exception to this is the case in which those legal structures restrict the prior claim of God's will in the life of the Christian. Then, like Peter in the early church, it is the Christian's responsibility to obey God rather than man. But when the laws of man do **not** run counter to the laws of God, it is our responsibility to be obedient citizens of the state. With respect to marriage, this means compliance with whatever blood tests, licenses, or other requirements may be a part of the law in a particular place at a particular time.

3. Physical Consummation

There is some mysterious way in which a husband and wife become one in God's plan. This is not only a spiritual union, but also a physical union. The wise man advises his son to "rejoice with the wife of thy youth" and "let her breasts satisfy thee at all times, and be thou ravished always with her love" (Proverbs 5:18, 19). The passage in I Corinthians 7:4, 5 (quoted above) is also an evidence of the necessity of the physical dimension of marriage love.

4. Spiritual Union

It is never in the will of God for a Christian to marry a non-Christian. That is not a Christian wedding and a minister committed to the principles of the Word of God will usually not want to be involved in performing such an unequal union.

Passages which speak specifically to this issue are found in Paul's two letters to the Corinthians. In I Corinthians 7:39 he reminds a widow that she may indeed marry if her husband is dead but that marriage may be "only in the Lord". It would be foolish to presume that somehow a Christian could marry an unbeliever the first time but the second marriage has to be restricted to "believers only". In the book of II Corinthians we encounter a passage frequently used to support ecclesiastical separation from apostasy and heresy. But the primary meaning of the passage seems to speak to the relationship of the husband and the wife: "Be ye not unequally yoked together with unbelievers; for what fellowship hath righteousness with unrighteousness, and what communion hath light with darkness?" (II Corinthians 6:14).

Christian Marriage is Based on Spiritual Love

Writing in *Christian Century* some years ago, Peter Bertocci emphasizes the fact that a marriage is not Christian just because the two primary participants happen to be believers. He warns that, ". . . this need not make a marriage Christian. Two married Christians do not make a Christian marriage. Their marriage is Christian only if the relationships and problems that their marriage creates are approached in the norms of Christian love." Clyde Narramore frequently reminds his readers that only that home is Christian in which Christ is fully acknowledged as Lord. The Greek word for love which appears in all of the marriage and family sections of the New Testament is the word **agape.** This word speaks of the kind of love that can only be produced in the heart of a person by the presence of God in the person of the Holy Spirit. It is the gift of the spirit in Galatians 5:22. It is the love of God for the world in John 3:16. It is the love of Christ for man in the epistle of I John. And it is the love of a husband for his wife in Ephesians 5.

Love is not some kind of ephemeral emotion which can be turned on to fit the occasion and turned off when not needed. As a matter of fact, it is not an emotion at all! It is an *attitude*. And until that attitude can be exhibited in maturity and recognition of its God-rooted origins as well as its family implementation, persons are not fully ready for Christian marriage in the Biblical sense. Marriage tends to be much more serious business than we recognize it to be. Our constant fault in evangelical churches is to allow our young people, sometimes even **push** our young people, into marriage too early, with too little preparation for the enormous task which lies ahead of them.

Christian love in marriage is better described than defined, which is precisely what Paul does in I Corinthians 13. In his helpful devotional booklet entitled *The Christian Home,* Dr. Gene Getz offers a quote from Henry Drummond condensing the positive description of Paul's emphasis in verses 4-7 of I Corinthians 13:

> This spectrum includes nine ingredients: Patience, kindness, generosity, humility, courtesy, unselfishness, good temper, guilelessness, and sincerity. When these characteristics are present in the life of the Christian, Paul says he is manifesting "love."

Christian Marriage Observes A Commitment To Biblical Principles

In one sense everything that we have looked at so far in this chapter can come under the category "Biblical Principles." But apart from the issue of purpose, definition, and marital love, there are some generalized principles which pop up here and there in the text of Scripture and are sometimes overlooked in our thinking about Christian marriage. In the fullest observation of the principle of context in Biblical interpretation, the entire Bible is the context for our understanding of any given doctrine, and consequently for our understanding of the "doctrine" of Christian marriage. Here are four ideas which seem to be of significance in thinking our way through what God has said on this important subject.

1. Marriage is Not For Everyone

Our society (even among evangelical Christians) has rather cruel attitudes toward persons who have passed "marrying age" and . . . yet have not linked themselves to a partner. It just seems improper for a person to go all through life single and we make up jokes about "old maids" and do very little planning for educational and social activities in our churches for people who are in the adult age bracket, but not in the ranks of the married. But it is not the will of God for everyone to take a wife or a husband. No doubt marriage is the predominant pattern, but it is not the exclusive pattern of God's plan. Paul wrote to the Corinthians,

> But to the unmarried people and to the widows, I declare that it is well — good, advantageous, expedient and wholesome — for them to remain (single) even as I do.
> My desire is to have you free from all anxiety and distressing care. The unmarried (man) is anxious about the things of the Lord, how he may please the Lord; but the married man is anxious about worldly matters, how he may please his wife. And he is drawn in diverging directions — his interests are divided and he is distracted (from his devotion to God) (I Corinthians 7:8, 32-34b, *The Amplified Bible).*

Our Lord also spoke of those who made themselves eunuchs for the sake of the kingdom of God. Perhaps we are to interpret that passage not in the terms of voluntary sterilization or voluntary celibacy as much as a symbolical commitment to the cause of Christ. The work of the church substitutes for a commitment to one's spouse and family. It may be a minority position to serve Christ in the role of a single person, but it is nevertheless a very Biblical position, and one that should not be abused and made light of by others who happen to be called by God into the majority group.

2. Marriage is For Two People Whom God Has Called Together.

The companionship concept is mutual. The voluntary agreement to live together as husband and wife must be based not only on physical attraction or the happy complementing of personalities. It must be based rather on a clear understanding that "God has brought us together" for the purpose of establishing a Christian home. But how does one ascertain the will of God on an important matter like this? The answer is simple, and yet difficult. It is simple because one can say that the will of God on this subject is ascertained in the same way that it is understood on any other subject. It is difficult because a proper understanding of the will of God in any area is a matter which demands the best commitment to the Holy Spirit's internal message and the external truths of serious Bible study.

We surely must recognize that it is not the desire of our loving Heavenly Father to hide His will from us. He wants us to find His will and, therefore, will make every effort to communicate with us if we will only honestly seek that will. Missionary Dick Hillis has a quotation which he frequently uses reminding us that "God will not show you His will just to satisfy your curiosity." We might add that God will not show us His will until we are committed to doing that will whatever it might be. Unfortunately the issue of choosing a marriage partner is so fraught with emotion and romantic pitfalls that a clear understanding of what is the speaking voice of the Holy Spirit, is sometimes clouded by the palpitating rhythms of one's heart whenever he or she walks by. This is one reason why it is important not to rush into marriage. Sometimes a "cooling off period" for several months or a year leads to more mature judgment. An engagement period of reasonable length may give opportunity for reflection and honest consideration of what God is saying to us. Dwight H. Small writes in *Design For Christian Marriage*,

> There are no pitfalls to be feared when life's most important relationship is three dimensional from the earliest dating days, when Christ is the constant companion, the silent partner. The great business of our Lord is to lead each of His own to the one of His choice, and then along a successful and joyful path to that consumate day of Christian married oneness *(Design For Christian Marriage*, Revell, p. 221).

3. Marriage is For Adults Only
   The responsibility which marriage brings requires

maturity. The Bible never portrays marriage as a game or an experiment. There is no such thing as "trial marriage" in the mind or writing of God's authors. The maturity demanded is a broad, sweeping process which affects emotions, social sensitivity, mental development, financial solidarity, and certainly spiritual depth. To quote Bertocci again, "Let there be no mistake about it. Marriage can bring a terrible lonesomeness not known to the unmarried. What can be more horrible than two persons living day after day in the same space and yet never meeting at the point where life comes home to them?"

This is not to imply that no one can properly enter marriage until he is "mature". Maturity is more of a process than an event and one can certainly grow in all of these areas of maturity through the years of marriage. Indeed, nurturing and caring for marriage love is a primary task that the family faces. Those romantic fantasies soon fade in the nitty gritty reality 'of everyday family living. If the **agape** relationship between and among family members is going to last through the years it will last because it is fed and watered by those who want it to grow rather than stagnate.

4. Marriage is For Keeps

Jesus said, "What therefore God hath joined together, let not man put asunder" (Matthew 19:6). The issue of divorce is discussed in another chapter of this book but we must mention here that people entering Christian marriage must enter it with the recognition that it is a permanent relationship "till death us do part." In Romans 7 Paul uses this permanent relationship as an illustration regarding the role of the law in Christian living. Even as an illustration, however, he makes a point about the marriage bond: "For the woman that hath an husband is bound by the law to her husband as long as he liveth, but if the husband be dead, she is loosed from the law of her husband."

Sometimes we talk about marriage as being "eternal"

but that is not a Biblical concept. Jesus clearly said that there is no marriage or giving in marriage in heaven because our status there would be as the angels (Matthew 22:30). So marriage is indeed an earthly institution but is a symbol of heaven on earth if the requisites of Christian marriage are fully followed.

The early days of marriage are considered to be the best but that is an incomplete view. First, of course, comes a feeling of **exaltation** for the long awaited day has come and the moment of wedding vows is certainly a highlight of the life of any Christian. But then exaltation gives way to **excitement** because so many things are happening so fast. In fact, perhaps too fast. We might want to do some rethinking about the pressures that our social conception of a wedding puts on the young couple entering this enormously important state of matrimony. We could ease their opening hours by taking some of the stress off the formality of the ceremony of contemporary weddings. Then, of course, there is the level of **enjoyment** as *all* the joys of marriage are mutually shared. Soon comes a feeling of **encouragement.** The young couple are nodding their heads as veterans and saying to each other, "It's not nearly as tough as they said it would be." Adjustment to each other is working smoothly and some of the harder knocks of later years have not yet come.

Then comes the period of **enlightenment.** Some aspects of marriage cannot be taught no matter how many classes we offer or how many hours of counseling we require. These elements must be experienced and the experiencing is the only kind of education that will really work. Sometimes the experiences are extremely difficult, even heartbreaking. But they, nevertheless, contribute to the enlightenment that must be a part of the feeling of expectancy. Despite all of the wonderful things that have happened in the past, God has even greater things ahead of us because He brought us together for the purpose of companionship which we will share in deepening and more wonderful love until God decides to terminate it either by the death of one of us, or by the return of His Son, Jesus Christ for whom we joyfully wait together.

3

Roles and Relationships in the Christian Home

According to Dr. Paul Popenoe, respected founder and president of the American Institute of Family Relations, sound family life is the largest factor in mental health. He suggests that the "survival of the civilization depends on its being 'family minded'."

> The primary fact in this whole discussion is the existence of two sexes, male and female, which differ literally in every cell of their bodies. They will behave differently in almost any situation; they have and always have had different standards of value in large and important areas of life. A good marriage and a good family depend upon a man and a woman each of whom is a good specimen of his or her sex.[1]

The ridiculous performance of the contemporary Women's Liberation Movement is a demonstrable example of what excesses can be reached when human beings reject God's distinctive place for them in the scheme of home and society. Even in Christian homes today one of the biggest pitfalls on the path to happy family living is the distortion of Biblical roles for family members. Society, of course, has hopelessly distorted

---

1. Paul Popenoe, "Family Strength and Mental Health", *Family Life,* Vol. XXIX, No. 12, December 1969, p. 1.

the Biblical view through equalization of the sexes (a perverted role of the wife), television situation comedies (a perverted role of the husband), and an extreme overemphasis and almost glorification of youth (a perverted role for children). In the research (referred to in Chapter I, by Appel and Goldberg) the issue of role breakdown is viewed as a significant factor in the family crisis.

> They say also that every member of the family is to a certain extent "uncertain and/or unhappy with his role." Wives are not certain they really want to be wives and mothers, husbands are not sure they want to be husbands and fathers, and children are not given opportunity to experience true child life.[2]

In this chapter we want to look at four basic relationships of the Christian home. In order to assume these proper relationships the individuals involved must first accept their Biblical roles in the family structure.

Relationship of Husbands and Wives

The primary purpose of marriage is the fellowship of two adult people, male and female. The fulfillment of sexual needs, procreation, and the symbolism of spiritual relationships between Christ and the Church are important. They should never, however, be viewed in priority over the fellowship, companionship objective. In Genesis chapter 2 God decided that it was not good for man to live alone and made a helper who was fitting for him. From that day to this, all relationships in and of the Biblical home are dependent upon a satisfactory fulfillment of this primary relationship.

But what roles does Scripture delineate for husband and wife? Certainly there are many, but the limitations of this particular treatment restrict us to an examination of five roles of the husband and five roles of the wife. It is difficult to say that any of the roles is more important than any other except as Scripture

---

2. Gene Getz, *The Christian Home,* Moody Bible Institute, 1969, p. 1.

treats one to a great extent in accordance with the hermeneutical principle of proportion.

Biblical Roles of The Husband

1. A Biblical Husband Is A Lover

The Bible emphasizes this role in its physical, emotional and spiritual dimensions.

> And you husbands, show the same kind of love to your wives as Christ showed to the church when He died for her . . . that is how husbands should treat their wives, loving them as parts of themselves. For since a man and his wife are now one, the man is really doing himself a favor in loving himself when he loves his wife as a part of himself (Ephesians 5:25, 28, 33, *The Living Bible*).

The word in the original text is **agapao** which is the same word used in John 3:16 of God's love for the world. Of this word Tenney writes in his commentary on the Gospel of John, "It is the noblest and strongest in Greek. It connotes an act of the will rather than emotion, whim, or infatuation, and its measure is defined in terms of the result."[3] Other significant passages which relate to the husband's role as lover are I Corinthians 7:3 and Colossians 3:19. Our perverted society has confused masculinity with cruelty and harshness. Popenoe suggests that tenderness is particularly absent in American men and says, "Tenderness, in its many manifestations, between partners, and between them and their children, is indispensable to a successful home."[4]

2. A Biblical Husband Is A Provider and Protector

Paul wrote to the young Christian leader Timothy, "But anyone who won't care for his own relatives when they need help, especially those living in his own family, has no right to say he is a Christian. Such a person

---

3. Merrill C. Tenney, *John the Gospel of Belief,* Wm. B. Eerdmans, Grand Rapids, 1948, p. 89.
4. Paul Popenoe, "Towards Better Husbands", *Family Life,* Vol. XXIX, No. 6, June 1969, p. 2.

is worse than the heathen (I Timothy 5:8, *The Living Bible*). The Biblical pattern of male responsibility in marriage has always been one of caring for the wife and protecting her. Actually, the verses which specifically command this are few since the obvious nature of the responsibility seems almost to be taken for granted in godly marriages throughout both the Old and the New Testaments. The feminists who insist that behavioral differences in responsibilities between the sexes should be reduced and perhaps even eliminated are flying in the face of Biblical injunction regarding the husband's responsibility as provider.

3. A Biblical Husband Is A Teacher

The instructional role of the man in the home is another feature of godly family living which has been accosted from the earliest days of the organized nation of Israel. The Book of Deuteronomy (particularly chapters 6, 11 and 31) lays the foundation for home nurture in the Hebrew law. Paul was on good ground then, when he told the women of the Corinthian church to ask questions of their husbands at home if they wanted to learn something about the work of the church (I Corinthians 14:35). Too often, however, this rabbinical feature of Christian husbandship has been given over to the wife to perform either by default or by deliberate intention. In too many Christian homes today family devotions and prayer are accomplished only if the woman takes the leadership role. Husbands who allow this to happen are departing from the Biblical definition of their roles as teachers.

4. A Biblical Husband Is a Ruler

All arguments regarding the equalization of the sexes fade into nonsense when one looks into the Word of God. Peter reminded his readers of an Old Testament example:

> Sarah, for instance, obeyed her husband Abraham, honoring him as head of the house. And if you do the same, you will be following in her steps like good daughters and doing what

is right; then you will not need to fear. You husbands must be careful of your wives, being thoughtful of their needs and honoring them as the weaker sex. Remembering that you and your wife are partners in receiving God's blessings, and if you don't treat her as you should, your prayers will not get ready answers (1 Peter 3:6, 7 *The Living Bible*).

The quality of "headship" certainly refers to the deciding voice in the family but it is a deciding voice that must consistently produce a decision in harmony with Biblical principles.

5. A Biblical Husband Is A Priest

The relationship of husbands to wives delineated in Ephesians 5 is described as a parallel to the relationship between Christ and the Church. As her redeemer, Christ demonstrated love to the Church and bought her through the sacrifice of His own life. As her spiritual head He is responsible for conducting her affairs in accordance with the plan of Almighty God, and exercises, therefore, a very definitive priestly role. (Hebrews 2:17; 3:1; 7:24; 8:1). Although the writer of the book of Hebrews makes a clear distinction with respect to the pattern of Christ's priesthood following Melchizedek and not Aaron, it seems clear the intermediary function of the priest in representing man to God and God to man carries over to the husband's role in the home.

The League of Large Families headquartered in Brussels, Belgium, conducted an international survey among wives asking them to describe the most common failings of their husbands. The following seven emerged as those most frequently chosen:

(1) Lack of tenderness
(2) Lack of politeness
(3) Lack of sociability
(4) Failure to understand the wife's temperament and peculiarities
(5) Unfairness in financial matters
(6) Frequency of snide remarks and sneers at the wife in company or before the children.

(7) Lack of plain honesty and truthfulness[5]

The survey, of course, approached marriage and its responsibilities from a purely secularistic point of view, but it is interesting to note how many of the basic Biblical qualities, if properly carried out, would alleviate problems described by these wives.

Biblical Roles of The Wife

1. A Biblical Wife Is Encouraging in Her Relationship To Her Husband

There is an obscure passage in the Old Testament which pinpoints this quality of support which a husband always wants to find in his mate. It is found in the context of the wedding between Isaac and Rebekah. When the servant returns with the new bride Scripture records that "Isaac brought her into his mother Sarah's tent, and took Rebekah, and she became his wife: and he loved her: And Isaac was comforted after his mother's death" (Genesis 24:67). Now Isaac's "apron strings" relationship to his mother is a whole other story. The point is that Rebekah met a need in the life of Isaac: A need for security, companionship, and encouragement. Popenoe calls the absence of this quality "emotional non-support". He describes what I'm calling "encouragement" as "emotional security" and says,

> To a man, one of the main advantages of a home, is that it offers him a refuge from the troubles of the day. Life in the modern business or industrial world is not a picnic. He is fighting all day long, in one sense or another. When the whistle blows, he longs for peace, harmony, comfort, love. . . . . . The wife who creates that atmosphere in the home, who fills that place in her husband's life, knows her business![6]

---

5. Publication No. 138 from the American Institute of Family Relations, 5287 Sunset Blvd., Los Angeles 27, Calif. entitled *Seven Stumbling Blocks Ahead of Husbands*.

6. Paul Popenoe, *Are You the Perfect Wife?*, p. 354, American Institute of Family Relations.

2. The Biblical Wife Is Loving

A comparison of Biblical injunctions to husband and wife regarding love is most striking. Husbands are frequently commanded to love their wives, but wives are never commanded to love their husbands. The passage in Titus 2: 4, 5 is a third-hand reference to that love but not a command. Perhaps God built into the sexes emotional natures by which it is easier for a woman to love more consistently than a man who continually may have his attention distracted to business and other affairs. This, of course, does not mean that the wife should not love her husband. Indeed, her love is so strong that it is called "reverent" in Ephesians 5. In one area, however, there is an emphasis on the giving of love by the wife and that area is the physical or sexual part of marriage. Of course, here again, the injunction is two-fold in the pungent words of I Corinthians 7.

> The man should give his wife all that is her right as a married woman and the wife should do the same for her husband: for a girl who marries no longer has full right to her own body, for her husband then has rights to it, too; and in the same way the husband no longer has full right to his own body, for it belongs also to his wife so do not refuse these rights to each other (I Corinthians 7:3-5a, *The Living Bible*).

Perhaps the biggest danger to satisfactory sexual love is the mythical notion that sexual compatability is somehow fatalistic; that it either exists or it doesn't. Nothing could be further from the truth. Most sexual difficulties in marriage are psychological in origin and a willingness on the part of marriage partners to give of themselves in love to one another physically and emotionally is the only response to the passage above. Miles puts it this way.

> Thus, in the infinite wisdom of God, He willfully planned human life so that husband and wife could regularly express their love and commitment to each other through satisfying sexual experiences. These are designed to sup-

port, cultivate, nourish, fortify and keep fresh
personal love and devotion between husband
and wife.[7]

3. The Biblical Wife Is Submissive

The command to submit is the most oft-repeated
wifely injunction appearing in the pages of Holy Writ.
In the passage to which I keep referring, Ephesians 5,
Paul writes:

> Ye wives must submit to your husbands leadership in the same way you submit to the Lord.
> For a husband is in charge of his wife in the
> same way Christ is in charge of His body, the
> Church. (He gave His very life to take care
> of it and be its Savior!) so you wives must
> willingly obey your husbands in everything,
> just as the Church obeys Christ (Ephesians
> 5:22, 24 *The Living Bible*).

Several other passages support this emphasis (Colossians 3:18, I Peter 3:1, etc.) Just as consistent tender
love seems to be difficult for husbands, so the role of
submission and subjection is the common "hangup" of
Christian wives. Two common rationalizations are frequently heard with respect to this Biblical quality. The
first is the insertion of some kind of contingency ("If
my husband demonstrates genuine Christian leadership,
then I will obey him"). Of course, Scripture knows no
such distinction. In the third chapter of I Peter, the
apostle is speaking to women whose husbands are unsaved and the word rendered "subjection" in the Authorized Version is precisely the same word that is used
in the previous chapter for slaves and citizens of secular
government.

The second common rationalization is one of which
many Christian leaders seem to be guilty. Since the Biblical commands to submission seem so incongruous with
the democratic society of the twentieth century, there
seems to have been in recent years a gradual shift to

---

7. Herbert J. Miles, *Sexual Happiness in Marriage*, 1967,
Zondervan Publishing Co., p. 447.

the equalitarian emphasis preached by secular sociologists and counseling agencies. Grounds quotes Brenton from the *American Male* in describing the contemporary equalitarian pattern.

> What true equality means is the equal right to expression and growth, to be a person. It does not mean strict equality of leadership every time leadership is called for. It does not mean a rigid fifty-fifty kind of relationship between the marital partners, who place their lives, so to speak, on a scale to insure undeviating equality. It does not mean a constant and dangerous tussle for authority, in which each member of the marital pair jealously guards his territorial rights and watches anxiously for any undermining of this authority. **True equality entails a shifting, fluid, dynamic kind of interaction, in which leadership changes from one partner to the other depending upon their specific interests and areas of competence and on the specific contributions they're able to make in any given situation.** Leadership, dominance, and dependency—all shift with the particular needs and abilities of the marriage partners and with requirements of the situation.[8]

There is no question that the fifty-fifty marriage makes sense in terms of today's social mores and cultural values. It remains to be demonstrated, however, that such an emphasis can fit in harmony with the pattern of the Word of God. This is not to say that Scripture suggests that the husband is a brutal dictator in his home. The husband honors his wife as "the weaker vessel", loves her as a part of his own body, and her proper response is a regular submission to his leadership.

---

8. Myron Brenton, *The American Male,* N.Y., Howard Mc-Cann, Incorporated 1966, page 16, quoted in "The Changing Years," Dr. Vernon C. Grounds, unpublished monograph, distributed by the Conservative Baptist Theological Seminary.

4. The Biblical Wife Is Consistent and Stable

There is a lovely passage in the book of Proverbs which is too infrequently utilized in marriage counseling and discussion of family relationships. Without reproducing it all here, let us focus on just a few verses from Proverbs 31:10-31.

> The heart of her husband doth safely trust in her. vs. 11. She will do him good and not evil all the days of her life. vs. 12. Strength and honor are her clothing, and she shall rejoice in time to come. vs. 25. She looketh well to the ways of her household, and eateth not the bread of idleness. vs. 27. . . . let her own works praise her in the gates. vs. 31.

What a beautiful description of God's plan for the Christian wife! The 28th verse says that her husband and her children "rise up and call her blessed." And no wonder, since such industry and stability in a wife-mother are so rare in the barbarian society of these latter days.

5. The Biblical Wife Is Attractive

The Bible makes it clear that spiritual beauty is an internal and not an external quality. The dynamic passage in I Peter 3 describes inner beauty in verse four, "An unassuming and quiet disposition, which is in the sight of God of great price." Some women are failures as wives becasue they are first failures as women. Of course, the opposite may be true as well. The wise wife will want to make her husband proud of her in all things; not only her exploits with the cook book, but also her appearance in public. Not every husband wants his wife to be a beauty queen and, of course, that's fortunate. One imagines though, that the over-whelming majority of men desire their women to look, smell and act feminine.

In comparing the two lists above, you have noticed that only one word appears twice and that this is the word "love". There is no question that this is the key word in relationships between a husband and wife. Bertocci says that "love . . . is the law of growth in marriage. People who want to 'be loved' or 'love' only if they are approved and liked will find that marriage loses savor and becomes an insipid forced parade of mutual admiration".[9]

Happy homes take work and there is a constant danger of **stagnancy** in the love relationship between husband and wife. Some young people with the gleam of romance in their eyes think that if they get in contact with the right person and vibrations arise, all will be well till the end of time. Such immaturity only demonstrates a fearsome lack of readiness for marriage. Marital love requires nurture and care to not only survive, but grow to be more beautiful 20 or 30 years later than it was on the wedding day.

> They say a wife and husband,
> Bit by bit,
> Can rear between themselves a mighty wall,
> So thick they cannot speak with ease through it,
> Nor can they see across it, it stands so tall.
> Its nearness frightens them, but each alone
> Is powerless to tear its bulk away; and each
> Dejected wishes he had known
> For such a wall, some magic thing to say.
> So let us build with master art, my dear,
> A bridge of love between your life and mine,
> A bridge of tenderness, and very near,
> A bridge of understanding, strong and fine,
> Till we have formed so many lovely ties,
> There never will be room for walls to rise.
>
> (Anonymous)

Relationship of Parents and Children

After he clarified the first and primal relationship, that between husbands and wives, the Apostle Paul went on to say a few words about parents and children.

> Children, obey your parents; this is the right thing to do because God has placed them in authority over you. Honor your father and mother. This is the first of God's ten com-

---

9. Peter A. Bertocci, *Christian Century*, May 6, 1959, article entitled "What Makes a Christian Home?", p. 2.

mandments that ends with a promise. And this is the promise: That if you honor your father and mother, yours will be a long life, full of blessing. And now a word to you parents. Don't keep on scolding and nagging your children, making them angry and resentful. Rather, bring them up with the loving discipline the Lord Himself approves, with suggestions and godly advice (Ephesians 6:1-4, *The Living Bible*).

It is important to recognize that the word "children" here specifies **relationship** to parents and **not age.** This is the same word Christ used in the eighth chapter of John when he told the Pharisees that they were not Abraham's "children". No doubt many of the Pharisees were middle-aged and older. The point is they were not members of Abraham's family. The commands of Ephesians extend then to those who live under the roofs of their parents and are still legally committed to them for decisions and dependent upon them for support. Let's put it bluntly: for purposes of this passage teen-agers are children, though one would never use that term in our society to describe them.

The picture focuses even more clearly when we notice that the word **teknon** (rendered "children" in Ephesians 6) appears as "son" in many other places, including the parable of the Prodigal Son; the healing of the palsied man in Matthew 9; and the description of Timothy, Titus, and Onesimus in the letters of the Apostle Paul. The injunction to obedience is quite clear and is supported by Colossians 3:20 among other passages. Perhaps the key word in the relationship of parents and children is the word "unity" which tends at times to take on a frightening **shallowness** in contemporary society. The so-called "generation gap" is either an indictment of, or a threat to the Biblical relationship between parents and children.

This relationship is a total one not a description of two home teams divided by sex (father and son vs. mother and daughter). Evidence collected in research by Biller and Weiss confirms, for example, that "the father's particular relationship with his daughter seems very important in her sex role development. He may foster the establishment of a positive feminine identity by treating her as a female and encouraging her to behave in ways which are considered to be feminine by her "society".[10] Their research demonstrates that the father's attitude and relationship with the mother is a pattern but his relationship with the daughter directly affects feminine personality.

Relationship of the Family to God

The Biblical responsibilities of parenthood may be said to center in the word "Lordship". It is certainly no coincidence that the family life section in Ephesians 5 is introduced by the following verses:

> Look therefore carefully how ye walk, not as unwise, but as wise; redeeming the time, because the days are evil. Wherefore be ye not foolish, but understanding what the will of the Lord is. And be not drunken with wine, wherein is riot, but be filled with the Spirit; speaking one to another in psalms and hymns and spiritual songs, singing and making melody with your heart to the Lord; giving thanks always for all things in the name of our Lord Jesus Christ to God, even the Father; subjecting yourselves one to another in the fear of Christ (Ephesians 5:15-21 *American Standard Version*).

The common application of this passage in preaching and writing of commentaries is to general Christian behavior. But notice how relevant it is to the relationships within the Christian family and between the family members and their God. Read the passage again allowing the pronouns to relate to family members rather than just to believers generally. Mutually the family understands the will of God and walks carefully within it. Family members edify one another "in psalms

---

10. *Family Life,* Vol. 30, VII, July 1970.

and hymns and spiritual songs" and share together in thanksgiving to the Father. And mutually the family members subject themselves one to another in the fear of Christ.

Some may think such a suggestion is contradictory to early remarks about the subjection of wives to husbands, but in actuality the extended order of subjection is children to parents, wives to husbands, and husbands to God. There is a sense in which family members put down their own desires and interests for the sake of the other members of the family and to this extent they can be said to be in submission one to the other, and collectively, in submission to the Lordship of Christ.

The danger to this relationship is the ever present **sin** in individual lives. To the extent that the Word lays down specific commands for Christian family living, the violation of those commands becomes sin in the lives of family members. Wives sin when they do not obey their husbands. Husbands sin when they do not love their wives. Children sin when they do not obey their parents. And when the family collectively focuses its attention on worldly pleasures and materialistic concerns rather than their mutual love for and service of the Savior, sin begins to corrode the crucial relationship of the family to God.

Relationship of the Family to Society

The problems which contemporary society poses for the Christian family are described in chapter one. But here we must take a quick look at the other side of the coin. What impact can the Christian family make upon its society in the name of Christ? If the family is God's basic unit of education, might it not also be his basic unit of service and witness?

There are numerous evidences in Scripture that family units served God's purposes in history. Perhaps the outstanding example is that of Abraham. His influence on Lot and his spiritual preparation of Isaac to carry on the promise of the covenant indicate that Abraham's family was more than just a biological breeding ground for a new race. The Patriarch's value system led him to obey God to the point of sacrificing his son on the altar. Those people and leaders who befriended Abraham were blessed of God and the presence of his family brought enrichment through its testimony of the living God.

But all was not well at Abraham's house. Haagar could quickly tell us that, and Abimilech would have something to say too. Remember that there are no heroes in the Bible except God. Abraham was just a man God used despite his failings, his lack of faith, and his tendency to want to take matters into his own hands. Think of how the alien culture of his day could have worn down Abraham and his family. Sodom destroyed all of Lot's effectiveness for God so that even his own sons-in-law thought he was joking when he spoke to them of supernatural judgment. Far from allowing the world to pour him into its mold, Abraham was willing to be a pilgrim and a stranger marching to the beat of a heavenly drummer.

Another example of family training making an impact on society, is the demonstration of faith and obedience in the lives of the displaced children of the Bible. Remember the young maiden who told Naaman about the power of Elijah? Consider the courage of Shadrach, Meshach, Abednego and Daniel when faced by their captors with the potential destruction of their faith. David in the court of King Saul is another example. Where did these young people learn the devotion to Jehovah that was so essential at crisis moments in their lives? Surely the best answer to that question takes us back to look at their home life and what must have been strong parental adherence to Deuteronomy 6.

The Christian family sustains a relationship of witness in at least three distinct phases; first of all, its very presence and behavior in the community is an example of Christ and His church and a demonstration of the grace of God to all of those who know them and can observe their life. Secondly, the family actively witnesses together through the program of its church, through personal sharing of faith on the part of the family members, and perhaps through collective witness of one kind or another. Finally, the extension of family witness finds fruition as young people go out from the home, and like the displaced children of the Bible, carry their witness with them into various forms of Christian service or a multitude of other occupations and geographical locations.

4

Nurturing Children in the Lord

A recently released study conducted by the National Industrial Conference suggested that three out of every five families in this country will have a child living at home by 1980. To put it another way, the nation's parent population is expected to increase by twenty-three per cent during the 1970s, faster than during any comparable period since World War II. Not only will more people be parents, but the parents of the decade ahead will be younger, more affluent, and better schooled than parents of the past.

If this report is correct, then perhaps demographic trends will at last force the church to once again place the essential Biblical emphasis on the home as the primary educational agency of the Christian faith. Whatever possessed us to think through these many years that church educational programs could somehow substitute for the home in the task of Christian nurture, seems obscure as we face the failures that we've seen. Recent estimates suggest that a teen-ager will have viewed fifteen thousand hours of television by the time he graduates from high school, and Americans accumulate a total of nine years of television viewing at age sixty-five. Assuming reasonably regular attendance, that same person will have spent four months in Sunday school by age sixty-five. The pressures of mass media and secularized public education demand an all-out effort to resurrect quality Christian homes dedicated to the task of nurture.

Nurturing Requires Example

Children are incurable mimicks. When he was just five or six years old, my son spent several minutes in his parent's bedroom looking at himself in the mirror. Since this behavior is rather unusual for boys of that age, I waited to see what would happen next. Shortly he asked me to come into the bedroom and presented me with a question: "Dad, do I look as much like you as people say I do?" Hesitatingly I acknowledged a striking resemblance. Pausing for a moment to consider the matter he said, "I'm going to follow you around wherever you go so that when I'm older I'll look even more like you than I do now." That humbling experience directed my thoughts to a poem which I had heard many years before.

> A careful man I ought to be,
> A little fellow follows me.
> I do not dare to go astray
> For fear he'll go the self-same way.
> I cannot once escape his eyes,
> What e're he sees me do he tries.
> Like me he says he's going to be —
> The little chap that follows me.
> He thinks that I am good and fine,
> Believes in every word of mine.
> The base in me he must not see —
> The little chap who follows me.
> I must remember as I go,
> Thru summer's sun and winter's snow
> I'm building for the years to be —
> That little chap who follows me.

What many parents fail to realize is that the "passive" behavior which children observe in the home is very determinative of their character. *Christian Life* magazine in its February, 1966 issue, carried an article by a medical doctor entitled, "How Are We Imprinting Our Children"? The article describes experiments conducted by scientist Konrad Lorenz with baby ducklings.

The author points up that the little feathered babies will follow the mother duck with unhesitating obedience and that such committed following can only be learned during the first day or two of their lives. Furthermore, "if the mother duck fails to teach the young to follow her during these first two days, the duckling can be taught to follow another moving object like a block of wood", and the ducklings become emotionally attached to the object which they follow. McMillen suggests that human children are like ducklings in learning to follow parents, and that the "final impress that a child will carry through life is the composite of all the imprints that have been made".

> Today various specialists using human means are unable to stop the escalating statistics of crime, illegitimate pregnancies, hoodlumism, murder, and lawlessness. These increases are clearly related to parental failure to imprint their offspring with God's admonitions. Mother's and father's begin too late and do too little to keep their children from being branded with searing literature, jazz, and the perverted sex concepts which are all condoned because "everybody is doing it".[1]

The child's home environment affects every aspect of his life, both while he lives in the home and long after he leaves it. In earlier pages, we have already suggested that the examples of his parents, positive or negative, will form the child's own role as a parent when he comes to that point in his life.

Nurturing Requires a Climate of Love and Security

In Colossians 3:21 Paul writes, "Fathers, provoke not your children to anger, lest they be discouraged". The need for these two characteristics (love and security) of a healthy personality is never outgrown but it is particularly crucial in the childhood years when the world all around seems so threatening. Children must

1. S. I. McMillen, "How Are We Imprinting Our Children?", *Christian Life,* Feb. 1966.

feel that they are wanted and welcome in the home. Domestic troubles, the fear of death, family quarrels, parental criticism, and even an over ambitious expectation of the child's performance can lead him to demonstrate symptoms of fear and insecurity. He can only feel safe in a strange, changing world if he always knows that despite his mistakes his parents will continue to love him and help him.

The aspect of the child's welcome in the home, of course, raises the question of birth control. In the absence of specific agreement and teaching many Christians are uncertain of the acceptability of birth control in its various forms. Yet it is regarded as generally practiced and general agreement among evangelical scholars indicates family planning through an acceptable form of contraceptive is within the lines of Biblical family living. Scudder has an interesting paragraph regarding this matter.

> Responsible parenthood demands planning the family. It is important for the Christian to have a positive doctrine of family limitation. A negative attitude with regard to a plan of control is not sufficient. Family planning should not be a matter of avoiding or suppressing, but rather a matter of properly employing the great potential of parenthood. It is necessary that all planning shall be within the will of God.[2]

In *Design For Christian Marriage* Small concludes, following a poll of "highly regarded leaders in evangelical ranks across America, . . . It would seem that in all wings of the church there is an accelerating acceptance of scientific contraception as a part of responsible Christian parenthood" (p. 107).

The basic danger of birth control is psychological rather than physical, although there are certain forms which raise serious questions about the health of the woman. Unspoken mental fear of what **might** happen

2. C. W. Scudder, *The Family in Christian Perspective*, Nashville: Broadman Press, 1962, p. 69.

is often more damaging than any physical results of most contraceptives.

Nurturing Requires Discipline

A proper concept of discipline has to do with the establishment of boundaries of behavior. This is true in the Christian life generally, as it is in the Christian home more specifically. A passage from Hebrews 12, although lengthy, is sufficiently cogent to warrant reproduction here.

> Think of him who submitted to such opposition from sinners: that will help you not to lose heart and grow faint. In your struggle against sin, you have not yet resisted to the point of shedding your blood. You have forgotten the text of Scripture which addresses you as sons and appeals to you in these words: 'My son, do not think lightly of the Lord's discipline, nor lose heart when he corrects you; For the Lord disciplines those whom he loves; He lays the rod on every son whom he acknowledges.' You must endure it as discipline; God is treating you as sons. Can anyone be a son, who is not disciplined by his father? If you escape the discipline in which all sons share, you must be bastards and not true sons. Again, we paid due respect to the earthly fathers who disciplined us; should we not submit even more readily to our spiritual Father, and so attain life? They disciplined us for this short life according to their likes; but he does so for our true welfare, so that we may share his holiness. Discipline, no doubt, is never pleasant; at the time it seems painful, but in the end it yields for those who have been trained by it the peaceful harvest of an honest life (Hebrews 12:3-11, *New English Bible*).

There are certain elements which must be found in home discipline if it is to be effective. Consider at least the following five:

1. Discipline Must be Consistent

There is little value to telling Johnny he must clean

his plate at dinner if such a mandate is only enforced two nights a week. It is the regular pattern of reward and punishment which produces a desirable behavior in the child. Many parents, for example, will verbally deny a child something he has asked for, only to give it after the child has vented his wrath in a temper tantrum, or nagged for the item until patience has been exhausted. To yield to this kind of behavior is, of course, to reinforce it and to teach the child that temper tantrums and nagging are efficient ways to procure desired items.

2. Discipline is More Than Punishment

Punishment is what must be used when discipline fails. If discipline is erecting the fences, then punishment is what happens when the fences are broken down, or when the child deliberately transgresses beyond the boundaries. Parents incorrectly conclude that a slap in the face is discipline. It is not. It is rather punishment, and probably a poor form at that.

3. Discipline is Based Upon Understanding on the Part of the Child

This is simply to say that a child must know where the fences are and why they have been put there. Certainly, in the early years of childhood, it is not necessary for parents to offer the child an explanation of everything which they ask him to do. Abject obedience is desirable at times, but more often an understanding of the rules will produce more satisfactory behavior.

4. Discipline Must be Applied in a Rational Rather Than an Emotional State

When little Susan comes home for dinner late for the third time in a row, mother's patience has crossed what Narramore calls "the threshold of frustrability" and she screams that Susan may no more go to play with that particular friend. In one sense, that dictum is punishment. In a very real sense, however, it is discipline, since mother has hastily erected a new fence without giving very much concern as to whether it is placed in a logical position at the proper time.

5. Discipline Should Lead the Child from Dependence to Independence

Unquestioning obedience is fine for small children. When a two-year-old begins to move toward a hot oven, one firm word from a parent should stop the child immediately without an explanation of the danger involved. As a child matures, however, and particularly in teen years, discipline should consist of an explanation of Biblical standards and an encouragement for the young person to make his own decisions considering his commitments to the Word of God, his understanding of the Holy Spirit's leading, and his assessment of the values and standards his parents have taught him.

Nurturing Requires Formal Instruction

A recent book by Cornell psychologist Urie Bronfenbrenner challenges the assumption that Americans demonstrate more concern for their children than Russian parents.[3] According to Bronfenbrenner, the attitude of Russian children toward teachers and parents is respectful, but affectionate. It results in a behavior which is attentive, mannerly, idealistic, and intellectually motivated. Bronfenbrenner's conclusion is that in America, the emotional vacuum left by today's loosely knit family is not filled in schools. Many Americans, he says, worry about their children, but very few really care for them and teach them. He suggests that what we need is more of what the Russians call, **vospitanie,** or *Character* education.

The Bible teaches that the home is a veritable school of Christian instruction. Paul wrote to Timothy, "Remember that from early childhood you have been familiar with the sacred writings which have power to make you wise and lead you to salvation through faith in Christ Jesus" (II Timothy 3:15, *NEB*). Church education is, of course, extremely important, but most severely limited unless it receives constant support from

---

3. Urie Bronfenbrenner, *Two Worlds of Childhood,* New York: Russell Sage Foundation, 1969.

the home. Joe Bayly suggests that "what our children (and we ourselves) need, is exposure to the whole Bible and its integrity, 'for doctrine, for reproof, for correction, for instruction in righteousness: That the man of God may be perfect, throughly furnished unto all good works.'" He decrys a lack of emphasis on the doctrines of law and sin and suggests that we focus more on a patient exposition of God's truth and less on the immediacy of the "decision."[4]

It is quite obvious to most Christians how the home and the church play strategic and complementary roles in the nurture of their children. The position of the school, however, is not quite clear. Obviously, it can be a support of a violent enemy. What is frightening is that many Christian parents have unhesitatingly abandoned their nurture responsibilities by default to the public school system. Dr. Robert F. Morrison, director of Cornell University's division of biological sciences, suggests that the family is a rather inadequate educational institution, and that teaching roles must be taken over by experts. The development of educational programs such as Headstart, he argues, testify "to the growing awareness that society, must, in effect, invade the sanctity or at least usurp some prerogatives of the home if it is to assure equal opportunity for all."[5]

I feel strongly that the nurture program of home and church should, if possible, be complemented by the nurture program of the Christian school. There is no space here to argue the case, except to say that the position rests on an understanding of educational philosophy and a Biblical concept of truth and value. Obviously, not every family can send its children to a school which will reinforce the theistic teachings of home and church. What is unfortunate is that many who do have this opportunity are ignoring it for very mechanistic and materialistic reasons.

4. Joseph T. Bayly, "The Teaching We Have Neglected", *Eternity,* January 1966, p. 17.
5. Robert F. Morrison, "Family Teaching Fails", *Arizona Republic,* Phoenix, Oct. 27, 1966.

Nurturing Requires the Cooperation of Husband and Wife

Family living is team work and it is essential for the leaders of the team to think alike on crucial issues. Mom and Dad must support each other's commands, rules, and discipline, even if at the moment it seems to one that the other is not making a wise choice. Any disagreements regarding family patterns and decisions should be discussed and prayed about together apart from the presence of the children. What the children need to see is a genuine love and mutual respect between their parents and among all members of the family.

It is also important for parents to spend time together with their children. Family vacations may make a significant dent in the budget, but the constant-to-getherness away from telephone and television may produce benefits far in excess of the cost. Family counselor Alma Jones reminds us that "scientific studies show that maladjustments of children decrease as family recreation increases; also that understanding and confidence between parents and children increase as shared activities and good times together increase.[6]

Nurturing Requires a Spiritual and Biblical Atmosphere of Family Unity

The Greek word which is translated as "nurture" in Ephesians 6:4, is the word **paideia.** The respected Thayer lexicon defines it as "the whole training and education of children which relates to the cultivation of mind and morals, and employs for this purpose now commands and admonitions, now reproof and punishment." The same word also appears in II Timothy 3:16 where it is translated "instruction". Here Thayer emphasizes the aspect of "intsruction which aims at the increase of virtue."

In the English language the word "nurture" is a

---

6. Alma H. Jones, "Fun With Children", American Institute of Family Relations, Publications No. 226.

botanical term often used to describe the activities of greenhouses in which tender plants and flowers are carefully grown to achieve the finest beauty and fruit possible. Obviously in a greenhouse the atmosphere is extremely important so that the young plant will receive just enough water and light to facilitate the growing process.

It should be clear that the spiritual atmosphere of the Christian home operates in precisely the same manner. The family should discuss spiritual things naturally, just as normally as they discuss the weather, school activities, or events around the house. The family should worship together regularly so that children view family worship as an integral part of living in the home, not something falsely superimposed upon real life. The family should also have fun together frequently. To quote Jones again,

> Because families tend to live more of their lives apart today, this is a matter of special importance since we are living in an age when moral leisure is taken for granted, some thought needs to be given to developing tastes in leisure, in a day when children intend to leave the home earlier, and go farther for their pleasure. For the young people to become inteligent consumers of what is offered in "bought" or commercial pleasures is largely a result of their experiences and attitudes formed in the home.[7]

Nurturing Requires a Communicaton of Proper Values for Life and Eternity

Isaiah once thundered the words of Jehovah when he told Israel, "My ways are not your ways, and my thoughts are not your thoughts. As the heavens are high above the earth, so are my ways above your ways, and my thoughts above your thoughts" (Isaiah 55:8,9). John reminded Christians who would read his epistle,

> Do not set your hearts on the godless world,

7. loc. cit.

or anything in it. Anyone who loves the world is a stranger to the Father's love. Everything the world affords, all that panders to the appetites, or entices the eyes, all the glamour of its life, springs not from the Father, but from the godless world. And that world is passing away with all its allurements, but he who does God's will stands forevermore (I John 2:15-17, *New English Bible*).

Throughout the history of man, God has made it clear in His revelation that Biblical values are not compatible with wordliness, materialism or temporalism. Christian parents should concentrate on nurture (instruction) which relates to the affective domain of learning, as well as the cognitive. That is, they should be just as concerned about the child's attitudes and value system as they are about the content knowledge which he accumulates. Too many children, indeed too many Christians of all ages, possess a reasonable smattering of knoweldge about Biblical facts, but have not yet mastered the art of translating the meaning of those facts into every day living. They are rather like the young boy from a rural area who had just completed his Bachelor's degree in agriculture. When asked if he was planning to continue in graduate work he replied, "Certainly not, I am not half the farmer now I know how to be."

Christian nurture in the home requires a consistent day by day inculcation of Biblical values which lead the child to the place at which he can volitionally make genuinely Christian choices on the basis of what he has learned. Then the words of Solomon will ring true: "The father of the righteous shall greatly rejoice: and he that begetteth a wise child shall have joy of him" (Proverbs 23:24).

5

Rebellion or Discipline?

In 1962 the radical Students for a Democratic Society was activated by a handful of students representing less than a dozen colleges. Now, just over a decade later, this leading revolutionary group claims 70,000 followers on 350 campuses who have established their principles and protests in visual and printed international media. In a recent *Newsweek* poll conducted by the Gallup organization the behavior of college students nationally was measured with respect to various controversial areas. The results: 50.8% had pre or extramarital sex relations; 36% had taken part in one or more campus demonstrations; 12.5% had broken the law as part of a protest; 31.9% had tried marijuana and 13.5% had used amphetamines. In the same poll the students rated their approval or disapproval of prominent American institutions. Organized religion edged out political parties by 33% to 18% approval but ran behind high schools, police, courts, Congress, business, families and universities. To put it another way, less than one-third of the students polled had positive attitudes toward the church.

But it is not the extreme radical fringe which poses the crucial problem for evangelical churches and Christian parents. It is the general attitude of rebellion which seems to be gripping the hearts and lives of youth and even children and turning them against authority figures

63

of all types. It is such a strange motivation that led a class of sixth grade students in upstate New York to respond to a substitute teacher's assignment by circulating a petition up and down the rows signed by those who refused to do the assignment.

The Distortion of Society

Behavioral psychologists promote the view that all a human being is or does is the result of external conditioning. His value system, life philosophy, and behavior are conditioned responses controlled entirely by his environment. Such a position is, of course, unpalatable to those who are familiar with the Bible's description of man, but in the process of rejection we dare not "throw out the baby with the bath water." Social standards and morals have a profound impact on the way young people think and act—even the young people from Christian homes.

Take the prodigal son, for example. Whatever the father and the elder brother may or may not have done to influence the life of this young man, it is quite clear from the way our Lord tells this story that the attraction of the world's distorted sense of values played a significant role in the rejection of his father's house and all that it stood for. He became a rebel not because he disliked his home or his parents but because the pull of worldliness and temporal pleasures overwhelmed his sense of loyalty. Like Demas, the bright lights of Thessalonica were too strong and the appeal to sensual appetites too demanding.

Psychoanalyst Bruno Bettelheim of the University of Chicago suggests that, "American parents and American society have not given today's youth the emotional equipment for engaging in rational and constructive protest." As a result, the violent and often irrational rebellion becomes a crude substitute for reasoned disagreement with adult values.

Perhaps one of the major themes of student rebellion is sexual permissiveness. It is rampant in all underground youth publications and exploited by movie makers and magazine editors the world around. Sexual perversion has historically been a dominant characteristic of social sickness and decline. According to *Time* magazine,

> At their fullest flowering, the Persian, Greek, Roman and Moslem civilizations permitted a measure of homosexuality; as they decayed, it became more prevalent. Sexual deviation of every variety was common during the Nazi's virulent and corrupt rule of Germany.

Youth rebellion may not be caused by society, but it certainly is encouraged by a general social permissiveness which creates and propogates the myths that society owes the rebel a living, that it will somehow provide him with happiness, and that it has the ability to meet his needs.

The Breakdown of the Family

Have you ever noticed that the Bible is an adult book, written by adults, for adults and about adults? There are five Greek words in the New Testament translated into some form of the English word "youth" or "young." In their entire collective usage the words appear only about twenty times. The reason is that God has ordained lines of authority and patterns of control in His world. The man is in subjection to God; the woman is in subjection to the man; the children (and youth) are in subjection to the parents; and the entire family is in subjection to the civil authorities which are ordained of God. When this system breaks down, the potential for rebellion is present. Furthermore, God has assigned to each family member certain roles and responsibilities. The father is to love, the mother is to submit, and the children are to obey. When these roles become perverted, the rebel nature rises and communication lines are cut between the rebel and all who do not share his point of view.

One of the classic cases of family breakdown leading to rebellion in Biblical history was in the home of Isaac. The young lad, Esau, was a skilled hunter, an outdoorsman of the first rank and such behavior captured his father's interest. On the other hand, the sensitive Jacob soon found that his mother was partial to him. The substitution of indulgence for love eventually drove the young Esau into the desert. A treacherous lack of discipline found mother helping one of the sons to cheat the father. In studying the account in Genesis 25 through 27 the only surprising outcome would have been if Esau had **not** become a rebel.

Why did Esau deem his spiritual birthright so lowly? Why hadn't he been taught by Isaac the profound significance of God's promise to Abraham? What kind of love was it that led Isaac to think of his son in terms of roasted deer meat rather than the program of nurture and edification so essential to all children? Didn't Isaac see in Esau a duplication of the problems with Ishmael? These are some of the questions which arise in examining the twenty-fifth chapter of Genesis for some clue to Isaac's failure in love.

On the contemporary scene, the lack of genuine love in the home leads to the deterioration of authority and control on the part of the father. In a most interesting book entitled *The Whole World Is Watching,* Mark Gerzon, a student activist at Harvard, attempts to explain the attitudes of the youth subculture.

> Perhaps the most influential reason for this generation's unrelatedness to the past is the change in traditional authority. The home in American society has become a dormitory. The father does not work at home, and, especially if he travels or works long hours or has a difficult shift, there is less contact between father and son. For children, father is someone who brings the money.

The seeds of rebellion are watered and fertilized in those early childhood days when the young boy wants to sit on daddy's lap and discuss his interests, regardless of how seemingly insignificant they may be. But dad has no time because the pressures of his adult world require him to invest his attention elsewhere. Ten years later, that father cries for his son's attention but it's too late—the birthright has already been despised.

Daniel learned his convictions well at home and was never deterred from his high and noble purposes. The three Hebrew children would rather die in the fire than rebel against what their parents had taught them to live for. Naaman's little slave girl had probably heard her parents speak often about God's power through his prophet.

But Isaac provided no such pattern for young Esau. As a matter of fact, Jacob's performance as a father also bears negative witness to his home experiences. You see, the boys learned early how to lie and they learned it from their father (who incidentally had learned it from **his** father). It was shortly after they moved to Gerar when some of the local citizens asked Isaac about his wife and he responded by saying, "She is my sister." In spite of his sin, God in grace delivered him and prospered his family in Gerar but this incident provided a lesson in deception for Jacob who perfected the process even further. For Esau, it offered one more evidence that his home was not the kind of place he wanted to live in, nor his father the kind of man he wanted to be.

The Guilt of the Individual

Scripture teaches that human nature is basically selfish and proud. Left to himself, man rejects God and engages in the worst kind of brutality, as anyone who has access to newspapers can readily determine. Modern society lays the blame for inhumane behavior on psychological malfunctioning or more recently, on drugs. The hippie nomads involved in the infamous Sharon Tate multiple murder case were under narcotic influence at the time. American soldiers at the My Lai massacre had been smoking pot. But drugs actually magnify a state of mind and behavior which was already inherent in the individual. Jesus said, it is not what goes into the mouth that corrupts a man but that which comes out of the mouth because it is representative of his wicked heart.

The Bible is a book of realism. It tells about rebels as well as heroes. It tells about men whose hearts were wicked with the same accuracy used to describe men whose hearts were open toward God.

One of the dangers in focusing upon a generally guilty society is that it tends to push the finger of guilt away from one's own self. The Bible teaches not only **nostra culpa** (our guilt) but also **mea culpa** (my guilt). Paul rejoiced in the fact that Christ had come to save sinners but quickly added "of whom I am the chief."

Discipline has to do with the erection of "fences" which allow children and young people sufficient freedom to run and exercise their growing independence but still mark boundaries beyond which transgression will not be tolerated. It is not to be equated with punishment nor is it to be equated with a puritanical rage which screams moralizing cliches into the ears of young people every time they wander near the fences.

On the other hand, the total absence of fences encourages the young to wander away from the home until they ultimately become lost in the dark woods of rebellion. We get the impression from Genesis 27 that not only were fences not erected at Isaac's house, but the parents themselves contributed to the delinquency. With reckless abandon Rebecca says, "Upon me be thy curse, my son. Only obey my voice, and go fetch me them (the equipment to deceive her husband)." In the paragraph which begins at verse 18 we see Jacob emitting lie after lie in order to gain the blessing he so desired. For Esau this experience was the final blow. With a bitter cry, he turns against all spiritual and familial values and threatens murder. His rebellion has become complete; he has cut himself off from his family and his God and, in rank defiance of his father, he takes another wife from among the daughters of Ishmael.

How does the young rebel come to the end of himself? Or to put it another way, what can "unmake" a young rebel? The answer lies in a treatment of the causes. The rebel recognizes and confesses his own guilt, returns to a position of sonship and obedience in the family, and rejects the distorted value system of society. This is, of course, precisely what the prodigal son did when the Scripture records, "He came to himself." In the words of *The Living Bible,* he said, "I will go home to my father and say, 'Father, I have sinned against both heaven and you, and am no longer worthy of being called your son'." And as in the parable, so in real life, every father who is properly exercising that role will welcome and restore the returned rebel.

The Significance of Discipline

Discipline simply defined refers to the guidance of persons so that they learn to act toward family. friends, other persons and the larger society in an agreeable way. The close tie with the Biblical word "disciple" is not accidental and the instructional element of discipline is therefore obvious. The goal of discipline is the molding and strengthening of character by means of a clarification of behavioral guidelines and environment. Most important of all, discipline is not punishment. Punishment is what happens when discipline fails and too many of us confuse both the terms and the concepts by threatening to "discipline" a child by physical spanking or some sort of social deprivation.

Discipline in home and classroom must include the ingredients of wholesome and mature interpersonal relations. Foremost among those ingredients are love, acceptance, guidance, firmness, consistency, and an evidence of organization and discipline in the lives of parents and teachers. It should be obvious that love is not to be equated with doting nor firmness with threat. The behavioral fences need to be erected far enough out so that the child has ample room to exercise his physical, social and emotional attributes and yet close enough in so that the exercise does not damage the rights of others or the instructional progress of the group.

There are no simple answers to the multifold questions of discipline which raise themselves in every kind of home and school situation. The complexities involved force us, however, to continually search for new approaches to the whole matter of discipline. Some teachers adopt a rather naive attitude toward the matter by simply concluding that "today's children and young people are simply more incorrigible than those of previous generations" and then settle down to endure the inevitable discipline problems.

Though there may be, in the final analysis, no categorical answers to the question of good discipline, there certainly are certain basic approaches to the matter which will facilitate our understanding of how the application of discipline fits into the total teaching-learning process in the home.

A common cause of disciplinary problems has to do with the parents. Dad and Mom set the climate for the classroom and their attitudes and actions will elicit some kind of response on the part of the children. Sometimes when this response takes the form of discipline problems, the parent can only blame himself. He may be one who is easily irritated or overly sensitive and children react negatively to this. There may be inconsistency in promise or threat and sometimes just plain boredom. Either a constant hilarity in the home or a total absence of humor can lead to discipline problems.

There are certain general channels through which a parent may minimize the discipline problems in almost any family situation. For example, it is always necessary to deal with disorderly conduct quickly and firmly, and yet with genuine Christ-inspired love. No father or mother should ever forget the fact that discipline, like education, is a *process* and cannot be expected to "set in" overnight. The process of dealing with discipline problems begins with an analysis of the cause of the problem and only secondarily, an application of some solution.

In the final analysis, there are three kinds of discipline which might be delineated: enforced discipline, self-discipline and Christ-discipline. Unfortunately, we too often emphasize the first and forget that the whole process of education and growth is to lead children and young people to the second. The Christian, of course, will always be striving toward the third which is simply a bringing of the entire self under the control of Jesus Christ in conformity to the principles of the sixth chapter of Romans, a portion of Scripture which is very closely related to the whole subject which we have been discussing.

This chapter is sometimes referred to as the "right way of sanctification." It deals with the Christian's position and walk once he has become a member of God's family through faith in Christ. The four key words of the chapter are words of discipline and order in the individual life: know, reckon, yield and obey. These words describe a relationship to Christ as Lord and together create a doctrine of Christian discipline which serves as a model for all family members. A diagram of the concept might look like this:

Christian Discipline in Romans Six

Holy Spirit Operative in All

Obey God and
His truth,
vvs. 16-18

Yield your life to
God not to sin,
vvs. 13-15

Reckon (recognize and
realize) new life in
Christ, vvs. 11-12

Know that you are dead to
sin, vvs. 9-10

Steps Toward the Christ-Life

Such is the pattern of problem and solution. Discipline difficulties have both natural and supernatural causes. That is, one must consider environmental factors as well as sin in the life. By the same token these problems have natural and supernatural solutions and the wise Christian parent will apply them both.

6

Teen-agers and Their Parents

We live in a teen-oriented society in which nearly fifty percent of the population is under twenty-one. Yet the most common refrain heard from the teen ranks in the last two decades has been, "My parents don't understand me." Wilkerson cites a report by Science Research Associates which indicates that discipline is the chief source of friction between parents and children. With regard to nurture the report states,

> Ninety percent of the teen-agers said that they looked to their parents for instruction in what was right and wrong but that their parents did not always fill this need. Only about half went to their parents with their personal problems, the same number said they did not think their parents understood their problems. Quite a few indicated that they felt their parents withheld advice because they thought the youngsters did not want it.[1]

There has been a great deal of discussion in the sixties about the so-called "generation gap". Some of us, however, believe that there is not a generation gap at all. The very terminology suggests that the problem is chronological. Yet the same fifteen-year-old who complains that he can't speak to his thirty-seven-year-old

1. David Wilkerson, *Parents on Trial,* New York: Hawthorn Books, 1967, p. 50, 51.

father seems to have very little difficulty relating to a thirty-nine-year-old high school guidance counsellor. Perhaps we could suggest that the "generation gap" is really a "communication gap", and that communication between teen-agers and parents is based on: (1) the willingness of the teen-ager to accept a Biblical role in the home (2) the willingness of the teen-ager to accept the necessity of a family context for growing up (3) the necessity of the teen-ager to accept himself with sufficient respect and understanding.

What Does the Bible Teach About The Relationships of Teen-agers to Parents?

Scripture always suggests a team concept of the family emphasizing that the whole is greater than the sum of its parts. Since the Bible is an adult book, it is somewhat difficult to find passages that deal specifically with teen-agers and perhaps the best picture can be drawn by looking at the lives of some of the young people that God dealt with.

David was a young man in a large family who learned early the role of obedience to his parents and respect for authority. When Samuel came to seek a king at the leading of Jehovah, Jesse never even considered that the young, shepherd boy out in the field could qualify. When Jesse said, "Go down to the camp and take this food to your brothers," Scripture records that, "David rose up early in the morning, and left the sheep with a keeper, and took, and went, as Jesse had commanded him" (I Samuel 17:20, *ASV*). Arriving at the court of Saul (probably after the Goliath episode), David was immediately noticed. It was reported that he was a young man skillful in playing, a mighty man of valor, a man of war, prudent in speech, a handsome lad, and that Jehovah was with him. What a testimony David's young life had already become! His obedience and faithfulness to both father and king were doubtless a result of his prior commitment to Jehovah.

Daniel learned his convictions well at home and,

when he arrived in captivity, he "purposed in his heart that he would not defile himself" with the life style of the heathen Babylonians. His pattern of daily prayer was so well established that even the threat of death could not alter it.

Joseph never forgot his standard of holiness. One could hardly point to his family life as expressing a Biblical ideal, yet somehow despite a sneaky, cheating father and cruel brothers, Joseph remained tender-hearted toward his God. When he was taken down to Egypt, Satan brought before him the sin situation which has caused failure in may of God's choice young men throughout all of history. The secret was Joseph's recognition that such a sin would not only be a sin against Potiphar, but primarily and ultimately a sin against God (Genesis 39).

Timothy became a Bible student early in life and knew no wasted years. It is true that he could never get up in a testimony meeting and tell a dramatic conversion story about being redeemed from the depths of alcohol and immorality, but his story was one of **even greater grace;** namely that God never let him slip to those depths in the first place. His leadership in the early church was grounded in years of listening and obedience to the teaching of his mother and grandmother who urged him to follow Christ's example through the years of his youth.

Most of the experiences which the Bible records about these four young men did not happen while they were teen-agers. Nevertheless an obvious commitment to parental authority and teaching during childhood and teen years produced its healthy fruit in adulthood. Remember that the Bible is an adult book, written by adults and for adults. The reason some flamboyant youth evangelists have to play exegetical and hermeneutical games to find preaching texts is that God has ordained the home to be the center of nurture for teen-agers and gave us the Bible to show adults how they should shoulder that responsibility. Consequently, obedience is a Biblical requirement which remains binding as long as the young person lives under his parent's roof.

What Needs of Teen-agers Are Best Met in A Family Context?

One can answer this question with a very long list of items detailing almost every aspect of teen life. The following have been chosen because they are four which are so flagrantly violated in contemporary American society.

1. The Family Can Provide Patience and Understanding Regarding Problems and Changes

The years of adolescence bring many changes in the life of a teen-ager, both in his own body and in the world around him. During these years the teen-ager wants desperately to be more grown up than he really is and he sincerely desires independence of adults. Peer pressure is strong, and young people develop loyalties to other teens and their ideas. Attraction to the opposite sex begins and the young person becomes interested in personal traits and appearance, seeking social approval and attempting to identify a distinctive place in a fragmenting society. Intellectual ability is increasing and the vast store of knowledge begins to unfold and threatens even to engulf him. In later adolescence individualism sets in and special interest groups develop. Soon he will be faced with choosing a life mate and vocation. Soon also he will break away from the family circle and, strange as it may seem, the success and satisfaction of that break will be largely determined by the way the family itself has prepared him for it.

2. The Family Can Provide Authority and Controls to Curb Rebellion and Lawlessness

The doctrine of original sin is violently opposed in the secular society and even many Christians raise a questioning eyebrow when told that man comes into this world with "a bent toward sinning". The Scripture is clear on the matter. David wrote, "Behold I was brought forth in iniquity; and in sin did my mother conceive me" (Psalm 51:5, *ASV*). And David's son, Solomon, wrote to his many grandsons: "Foolishness is bound in the heart of a child; but the rod of correction shall drive it far from him" (Proverbs 22:15).

Christenson bemoans the deterioration of the concept of original sin in a most effective volume on the Christian family:

> Two World Wars, followed by a generation of cold-and-hot wars, have somewhat tempered this naive optimism regarding human nature. Yet many of our unconscious pre-suppositions and judgments are still based on the idea that human nature is basically good, for this idea has penetrated every area of our culture and thinking. And not least the area of child raising! Much of the grief in parent-child relationships is rooted in this false understanding of human nature. Parents look upon their children as basically "good". When they show up "bad" in a particular situation, the parents begin to search frantically for the reason: "What is hampering and restricting my little angel, that he should do such a thing?[2]

The innate rebellion and lawlessness which Satan causes in the hearts of men shows itself during the teen years in rather definite ways. The clearcut propensity toward disobedience, strong-headedness in pursuing one's own way, the desire for promiscuous sex, and the whole philosophy of "do-your-own-thingism" stems from the false humanistic notion that the sixteen-year-old now has the authority to run his own life. Most parents of today were alive in 1947 when Jackie Robinson became the Brooklyn Dodgers' slugging and running second baseman, the first Negro in professional baseball and Rookie of the Year as the Dodgers grabbed the National League pennant. Twenty-one years later in March of 1968 Jackie, Jr., was bailed out by dad at Stamford Circuit Court (Connecticut) having

2. Larry Christenson, *The Christian Family,* Minneapolis, Minnesota: Bethany Fellowship, 1970, p. 95.

been arrested for possession of marijuana and heroin. In explaining his failure as a father, Jackie, Sr. said:

> I guess I had more of an effect on other people's kids than I had on my own. My problem was my inability to spend much time at home. I guess I thought my family was secure, that we didn't have anything to worry about, so I went hunting around everywhere else.

When a reporter prompted Jackie about his great successes in reaching hundreds of underprivileged kids in ghetto areas, Jackie mused, "Well I don't know, I find it pretty difficult to find how I can reach other kids but I can't reach my own." Parental indulgence is a major cause in facilitating the rebellion of teens. The major outlets of this rebellion are illicit sex and immature marriage, both of which are increasingly pressing problems, even among evangelicals in contemporary society.

3. The Family Can Provide Security and Love to Combat the Confusion of Fear of Society

Certain aspects of group behavior and certain facets of instruction can only be learned in larger group settings such as a school. On the other hand, small groups offer teen-agers significant opportunities to advance the process of maturation. But neither schools nor peer groups can provide genuine love and security. Such emotional therapy is best received in the family contexts and few substitutes are available.

4. The Family Can Provide Sex Education

Here is an area which the family has given over to other agencies by default. Teen-agers will get sex education; the only option is, where? Should it be given in the school? Probably. For non-Christians, secularized sex education is better than none at all. Should it be given in the church? Certainly. Since the sexual aspects of human behavior are part of the whole of man, and since it is the responsibility of the church to train the whole man, the church has a responsibility for communicating a Biblical attitude toward one's sexual nature. Should it be given in the home? Obviously. The context of love and security makes the home the best situation for sex education even though the teachers there may be the least trained.

What About Dating and Going Steady?

Wholesome dating experience for Christian teen-agers must be encouraged. Parents have responsibility for teaching the "what", "who", "when", and "how" of dating. Dating relationships must be based on personal convictions and self-imposed standards but the convictions and standards are at least partially the result of parental instruction.

Christian teens must also be taught the influence which they have on members of the opposite sex. Years of working with Christian college students has led to the conclusion that the first eighteen years provide Christian young people very little information on how members of the opposite sex react to their sight and touch. Christian mothers need to teach their teen age daughters restraint in the use of the explosive power which they possess to "turn on" boys and men. Style of dress and manner of behavior are crucial in maintaining a life of Christian modesty.

Young men need to be taught by their fathers how to behave as gentlemen in handling the affections and delicate emotions of the girls they date, and particularly those with whom they "go steady". And, of course, this raises another question. What about going steady? The condition is sometimes called "premarital monogamy". Surely there are arguments in its behalf since kids have been doing it for decades. It provides the security of a ready date whenever it is needed and supposedly each can depend on the other's romantic commitment. Also, it certainly gives the teens opportunity to know each other well before engagement for marriage is suggested.

Many, however, would argue that the negative effects of going steady far outweigh the benefits. They believe that it leads to promiscuous activity among teen-agers. Abigail Van Buren (certainly no fundamentalist preacher) prints with approval a letter from Houston, Texas.

> Dear Abby: I have always cheered when you encouraged mothers to build the kind of relationships with their daughters that will enable them to have good frank talks. DON'T QUIT, Abby. It is so important.
>
> I work for an adoption agency, and until parents realize that "going steady" usually leads to going "all the way" we will continue to do a booming baby business.
>
> At least 95% of our girls are pregnant by their "steadies."
>
> I wish every parent who has a daughter "going steady" could sit beside me for one day and hear all the misery and heartache reflected in the conversations with girls who are giving up their babies.

Another problem of "going steady" is that it tends to lead to early marriage. Judge R. Milligen, Jr. of the Stark County Juvenile and Domestic Relations Court in Canton, Ohio, laments the fact that the marriage age is steadily getting lower.

> "Playing house" is fun—for a while—but marriage in the Judeo-Christian concept requires much more than a juvenile, physical attraction and camaraderie. Every adult is aware of the fierce competition for jobs and the increased technical proficiency required to perform in industry and business today. Yet despite the employment facts of life the number of teen age marriages continues to increase in an alarming number.[3]

Dr. M. J. Hungerford suggests that "millions of Americans marry before they are really ready to undertake the responsibilities involved, and these teen age weddings lead, half the time, to failure and divorce." She goes on to list eight areas in which progress needs

---

3. John R. Milligen, "As Viewed from the Bench" unpublished pamphlet distributed by The Plain Township Puritan Club, Canton, Ohio, 1964.

to be made in properly preparing teens for marriage.[4]

(1) Home, school, and community agencies of all sorts can help youth to understand the value of education and plan deliberately for careers.

(2) These same agencies, in short the totality of our culture, must come to grips with the fundamental problem of what sexuality is for.

(3) A crucial part of this task is to make clear the meaning of **love,**—one of the most misused words in the language.

(4) A realistic picture of what is required to make a good marriage . . .

(5) . . . A realistic understanding not merely of love and marriage, but also of parenthood.

(6) School, church, and community agencies (e.g., boy's and girl's clubs) can do a much better job in helping youth to understand their own parents.

(7) Young people desperately need not merely general education but individual guidance . . .

(8) Along with all this, effective ways must be found to give all young people more active and meaningful contact with the world outside of their own homes and classrooms.

How Can We Offer Family Life Education To Teens?

We can start by impressing them with the seriousness of marriage and the kind of thorough preparation that is necessary for a successful marriage. There are certain Biblical principles for Christian marriage which are absolute and in violent contrast to the loosening standards of society. Such teaching is no small task in the seventies because the society has its own instructional system which inculcates relative morals and relative value systems for thirty or more hours a week. Evelyn Duvall emphasizes the significance of premarital behavior.

---

4. Mary Jane Hungerford, "Preventing High School Marriages", *Family Life,* Vol. XXVIII, No. 9, (Sept., 1968): 1-3.

Years ago it was discovered that there was a direct relationship between premarital conduct and marital happiness. More husbands and wives who had not had sex experience before marriage were happily married than those who had. Men and women who have been permissive sexually before marriage cannot be expected to change miraculously when they marry. With few exceptions, they continue to manage their sex impulses as they did before they married. If adultery would not be serious to you, then premarital chastity may not matter so much. But if fidelity in marriage is important to you, then recognize that it is tied in with fidelity before marriage.[5]

For the Christian young person premarital unchastity is more than a danger to his or her future and an act of selfishness. It is an act of sin against God because God's standards of behavior apply in all situations and at all times.

Christian teen-agers also need to learn the Biblical perspectives of the human body. How many Christian moms and dads genuinely spend time with their children and teen-agers teaching them about menstruation, nocturnal emission, homosexuality, and masturbation? Yet these are crucial and pressing issues in relation to one's body. Recently I heard that the teen age daughter of a Christian friend told friends she was offended because her pastor called homosexuality sin and she knew full well from what she had been reading about the subject that it was a disease. Such immaturity with respect to the Biblical position on homosexuality is a common occurrence among Christian teens.

The general principle that undergirds preparation for marriage is a complete commitment to the will of God. Teen-agers should not be frightened into believing that God has just one person for them to marry and, if they miss that choice, they have completely missed

5. Evelyn M. DuVall, *Why Wait Till Marriage?*, New York: Association Press, 1965, p. 87.

God's blessing for the rest of their lives. Such neo-Puritanism is a gross injustice to the loving nature of a God of grace. Rather they need to be taught to live in the constant control of the Holy Spirit and an understanding of God's Word so that the Spirit can lead them in choosing dating partners, in responding to offers for dates, in behavior with boyfriends and girlfriends and, of course, the ultimate selection of a marriage partner. There is an old motto which is just as true today as when it was given and has worked through the years in the lives of hundreds of teen-agers: "God always gives His best to those who leave the choice to Him."

7

Pop Rock and Christian Teens

How many a Christian parent has rushed in terror to his teen-ager's room frantically grabbing the volume knob on the portable radio that seemed like such a good idea for a Christmas gift just a few weeks ago. The thing that bothers him more than anything else is how his pride and joy, raised these many years in a loving home and evangelical church, can sit, or stand, or jump, or wiggle by the hour, snapping his fingers and stamping his feet to what seems to dad like the offscourings of a Mau Mau Mardigras. But it's what's happening! *Look* magazine says teen groups "go up so fast, they're the uncountables. Over 200 new records push for attention every week. Kids must have new sounds. Guitar players you never heard of make $70,000 a year." And Christian teen-agers who are not affected by the pop rock craze of the 1960s and 70s are harder to find than a rock guitarist without an amplifier.

What is Pop Music?

That question is considerably easier to raise than it is to answer. As we use the terminology today, "pop music" is a broad category into which almost all commercial types of music would fall. It is certainly not used in the context of former decades when music by the Boston "Pops" meant light classical overtures and creative musical scores such as those written by LeRoy

Anderson. What is happening, of course, is that America's music is reflecting its culture. According to Niebuhr, "Culture is the artificial, secondary environment which man superimposes upon the natural." The point is that although we would like to believe that the church is constantly making an impact on its culture, we must honestly recognize that contemporary culture also makes a profound impact on the church, and as far as music is concerned, particularly on its teen-agers.

The focus of this chapter is not therefore, on classical music, show music, ballads, blues, or even progressive jazz. All of these have a significant role to play in the culture of the twentieth century, but the music which is making an impact on teen-agers in the decade of the 70s is "pop rock," or what might be called "teen-feel music."

That kind of descriptive jargon derives from the practice by commercial record companies of beaming their material to the young teen age group. Pop rock is not as vogue with the college crowd today as it is with junior high. Most college students reject the screaming, screeching amplifiers in favor of either folk or folk rock.

What is most disturbing about the whole problem is that sociologists and anthropoligists are probably correct in telling us that man's music reflects what he really is. With its constant emphasis on lust, selfishness, and eroticism, pop rock gives evidence of the fact that man is a hopelessly fallen creature whose life is lived as far away from holiness and communication with God as it could possibly be. In this kind of a matrix the commands of Christ still echo down the halls of history:

> I have given them thy word; and the world hath hated them because they are not of the world, even as I am not of the world. I pray not that thou shouldest take them out of the world, but that thou shouldest keep them from the evil. They are not of the world, even as I am not of the world (John 17:14-16).

Whatever else it might be or not be, pop rock is certainly the loud and obvious representation of a psychedelic society.

Why Do Teens Listen to Pop Rock?

Look magazine quotes one teen-ager as saying,

There is nothing else like it. You come home from school all beat up and tense, and that night you go to a dance and you let go, and you get home feeling really good. For instantaneous effect, nothing can beat rock, because it's right there, it's not hiding anything, it's hammering everything completely into you.

It is legitimate and perhaps even necessary to raise the question of the impact of lyrics versus beat in the attraction of pop rock. Some Christian parents, for example, argue that rhythm is rhythm and the rhythm of pop rock is no worse than the rhythm of a Strauss waltz. They bolster this argument by suggesting that their teen-agers pay no attention to the words and are really only interested in the beat. Nothing could be farther from the truth. Most teen-agers know every word of the hit tunes at the top of the charts in any given month.

An analysis of the lyrics, furthermore, indicates that in most cases they are frankly suggestive. What used to be harmless puppy love has now become outright eroticism. The 1960s, for example, produced lyrics like the following:

"When we are dancing and you are dangerously near me, I get ideas."
"I have mixed emotions when it comes to loving you. I know I shouldn't like the things you shouldn't do."
"Go away little girl before I beg you to stay."
"Young girl get out of my mind, My love for you is way out of line. You better run girl; you're much too young girl."

The late 60s brought an even more complicated problem. Many of the titles and lyrics being produced then had hidden meanings understandable to many teen-agers familiar with the code of the in-group, but totally indiscernible to parents. It's quite possible, for example, that songs like "Lucy in the Sky with Diamonds," "Green Tambourine," "Mr. Tambourine Man," and "Judy in Disguise" are songs which glorify the use of narcotics and drugs; and constantly reinforce active rebellion and hostility towards parents and others in authority.

Bob Larson, former rock and roll guitarist before his conversion, is vociferous in his utter condemnation of the effect of rock and roll. In speaking of the matter of words he suggests that,

> Lyricists fancying themselves to be poets, are using existential themes of life, death, loneliness, alienation, and existence. War, the pill, drugs, and promiscuity are all part of the music that is a complete expression of its time and audience. Songs like 'Sock It to Me Baby,'' "Baby Light My Fire," "Hungry for Your Love," "Let's Spend the Night Together" have obvious lustful and erotic lyrics.

Many pop artists don't even attempt to hide the fact that the lyrics of their music have definite hidden meaning. In the Peter, Paul, and Mary tune, "I Dig Rock and Roll Music," one verse frankly tells us, "I dig rock and roll music, I could really get it on in that scene, I think I could say somethin', if you know what I mean, but if I really say it the radio won't play it, unless I lay it between the lines."

In the same way that small children crave constant attention and want their parents to be near them and with them all the time, so teen-agers are sensing their innate need for independence and wanting to exercise it at every turn. Since adult rules and standards often conflict with a teen-ager's idea of what ought to be happening, he finds himself in confrontation with his parents and other adults at many times during his teen years.

Furthermore, pop rock tends to reinforce this attitude

of rebellion and supports a premature independence from adults. This is done through a number of things, but primarily through the love-sex theme which advocates early maturity through a presentation of adult situations.

Most of the things in this world belong to adults. Teen-agers have a limited voice in politics, fashion, commerce, and many important aspects of life, but they know they rule the roost in the pop music field. Consequently, the teen-agers' desire for music of their very own, and the producers' willingness to give it to them if they will pay for it creates a vicious cycle of supply and demand. It's a little world in which adults have no part and teen-agers know it.

Adults aren't supposed to like rock music and teen-agers don't want them to like it. Often the very practice of listening to pop music is simply a way of creating a superficial delta between the teen and adult worlds.

Pressures and problems of the space age do affect our teen-agers. Most of the time they seem carefree and little concerned about the reality issues of life, but deep down inside they know what is happening and it frightens them. Furthermore, they are caught between the horns of dilemma and they want to avoid the hypocrisy and sham they see in the adult world; and on the other hand, they feel a desperate need for the hiding mechanisms which are a part of adult life. Howard Greenfield, a professional music producer, describes his philosophy in relation to this need: "What we do is take an adult idea and bring it down to the kid's level . . . a pop song is like a movie—it's a little escape."

What Should Christian Parents Do About It?

If the former two questions were difficult to answer, this one is virtually impossible. How nice it would be to offer a simple three step formula to wean your thirteen-year-old from the Beatles to Bach. Unfortunately, it doesn't quite happen that way. The problem with pop rock is that "everybody is doing it," and separation is the most unpalatable doctrine of the New Testament. Rock affects a teen-ager's physical senses, his emotions, and now even his intellect. Of the three, it most strikingly reaches the emotions and thereby has a profound effect on the decisions and attitudes of his entire life. The following suggestions are certainly not simplified solutions. They may, however, offer some semblance of guide lines by which we can begin to attack the problem aggressively.

1. Start Early to Build a Consciousness of the Problem With Your Children

Parents who want to rush into that bedroom and smash the portable radio when the son or daughter is already 16 and has been listening to pop rock for four or five years, are facing an almost insurmountable problem. He's already "hooked" and perhaps nothing short of the supernatural workings of a powerful God can release him at this point. The time to begin is when he first catches a glimpse of "American Bandstand" at the age of six or seven. He needs to grow up with an awareness of what pop rock is and what his reaction toward it as a Christian young person ought to be.

2. Face The Christian Teen-Ager With The Reality of What He is Involved In

Books like Bob Larson's *Rock And Roll The Devil's Diversion* tell it like it is. The teen-ager may resent this kind of confrontation because one of the reasons he is involved in pop music is an escape from reality. But the responsibility of that Christian parent is to show him that the Christian lives in contact with reality not hiding from it. No Christian teen-ager should be allowed to be caught up in rock "accidentally." If he chooses to involve himself, it should be with full recognition of what the issues are, and what the Biblical guidelines call for him to do.

3. Provide Satisfactory Identity Substitutes

Christian teen-agers who communicate well with their parents, are satisfied with their church youth groups, and keep company consistently with friends who share their faith in Jesus Christ, are less likely to get trapped in the pop rock web. One Christian teen-ager expressed it this way when asked why he didn't become a disciple of pop rock; "Who needs it?"

4. Seriously Consider The Issues When Determining The Family Rules

Pop rock music helps to drown out reality and also is a tool for dancing. It is not the purpose of this chapter to discuss at length whether dancing is appropriate for Christians or not. It must be indicated, however, that in our society teen age dancing and pop rock music are inseparably related. The argument that the partners touch or don't touch in modern dancing is irrelevant. The modern style of dancing and its shining prophet the discotheque are the clear expression of a persisting loneliness, lust, and desperation. The combination of sight, sound, and sex in the dance hall presents a convenient diving board for immoral activities on the way home. Larson suggests that parents who want to see a mass orgy in action should drop into a teen age rock and roll dance without warning. He suggests that modern dancing is no longer an artistic form of expression but rather a "subtle instrument of Satan to morally and spiritually destroy youth."

5. Keep A Dynamic Spiritual Atmosphere In the Home

If rock and roll and its various offspring are indeed representative of the god of this world, then the only force available for the Christian to combat this type of thing is the power of the Spirit within him and the power of the Word, the sword of the Spirit. The Christian home is a refuge and a training center for children and teen-agers. The spiritual love and guidance that ought to be a part of that home are our defense against the prince of the power of the air. It is in the home as well as the church where a Christian teen-ager learns to move positively after those things that will build up his Christian life and avoid those things which tear down and destroy the spiritual vitality within him.

The problem of pop rock and Christian teens is not

a question of legalism! We are not talking here about rules to hinder and hamper. Paul very clearly said as a Christian all things were legal for him, but not all things built up his spiritual life. Pop rock is the essence of immorality and Christian living is the essence of holiness. Pop rock talks about lust, and the Christian life talks about love. Pop rock is negative, and the new life in Christ is positive. Perhaps no better guide line can be given than that which Paul wrote to the young man Timothy:

And God's truth stands firm like a great rock, and nothing can shake it. And these words are written on it: The Lord knows those who are really his, and a person who calls himself a Christian should not be doing things which are wrong. In a wealthy home there are dishes made of gold and silver as well as some made of wood and clay. The expensive dishes are used for guests, and the cheap ones are used in the kitchen or to put garbage in. If you stay away from sin you'll be like one of these dishes made of purest gold—the very best in the house—so that Christ Himself can use you for His highest purposes. Run from anything that gives you the evil thoughts that young men often have, but stay close to anything that makes you want to do right. Have faith and love, and enjoy the companionship of those who love the Lord and have pure hearts (II Timothy 2:19-22, *The Living Bible*).

8

Teaching Convictions and Principles

The prevailing philosophies of the day are thoroughly steeped in relativism. We are told that all things are in a constant state of flux and the only thing sure is change. Nothing is true or real because tomorrow it might be proven false when judged by the changing, rapidly developing concepts of both natural and social science.

In the middle of this kind of world lives the Christian. Because of his faith he is chained to the concept that not all things are relative. There are some things which never change. The Word says, "Jesus Christ the same yesterday, today, and forever." Unable to rationalize Biblical absolutism with secular relativism, the Christian must develop a philosophy of life and a system of values which will equip him to live in a world which has thrown aside the unchanging truth.

Trapped in such a society thousands of Christian young people are traveling through the difficult land of adolescence without a road map. Their standards of faith and life are "secondhand" resting on the shaky basis of parental or church traditions. It is not sufficient when a Christian young person responds to a question of worldly behavior, "I don't do that because my mom and dad say I shouldn't," or "my church doesn't believe in it." He must stand before God as an individual able to give answers of the hope within him, not because of parental pressure nor because it is written in the articles of the church, but because the Spirit of God has led him to intelligent, Biblical, personal answers to the controversial questions of our day. Nothing less can endure in the rank materialism of American society today.

Christianity is not a religion of legalism. One of the few disappointments I experienced in ten years of teaching in a Christian college is confrontation with wonderful Christian young people who have been misguided into adopting oversimplified "do's" and "don'ts" in response to the difficult "gray areas" of Christian behavior. There are no "Christian laws" to govern the matters of dancing, smoking, theatre attendance, etc., but the Bible does provide clearcut guidelines for developing basic Christian convictions.

Guidelines For Biblical Convictions

The development of Christian convictions should begin with very small children; they can rarely be superimposed upon young people in colleges. The matrix for the development of Christian convictions is the home. From a dungeon cell in Rome Paul writes the very last epistle that he will ever write. He is soon to die but wants to remind his "son in faith" of the significance of his childhood faith.

> Timothy continue thou in the things which thou hast learned and hast been assured of, knowing of whom thou hast learned them; and that from a child thou hast known the Holy Scriptures which are able to make thee wise unto salvation . . . and is profitable for doctrine, for reproof, for correction, for instruction in righteousness, that the man of God may be perfect, throughly furnished unto all good works (II Timothy 3:14-17).

One can talk much about leadership training in the local church but the fact remains that such training begins in the nursery. The little events which build a life and form an attitude toward Christian service begin to be internalized just a few months after birth.

A second guideline reminds us that **the development of basic Christian convictions is a process and not an event.** Peter exhorted Christians in his day to "grow in grace and in the knowledge of our Lord and Saviour Jesus Christ." There are many crises in the Christian life characterized by decision experiences but as one seeks to live a life patterned after the life of Jesus Christ, he progressively develops in the process of sanctification.

When a person is saved, he just begins to live in Christ. The years of spiritual childhood are rich with learning experiences leading to Christian maturity. The person who is immature must either force some form of dependent legalism upon himself and others or reject almost all restricting standards. Because sanctification is a process, the developing of Christian convictions and standards is a process that runs concurrent with it.

The developing of basic Christian convictions must proceed from dependence to independence. There are a variety of disciplines in one's life. There is external discipline, self discipline, and Christian discipline. In college we see two common problems asserting themselves year after year. One is represented by the young person who comes from a home in which he was too soon passed on from dependence to independence. He was allowed to name his own way too early in life. He was permitted to make his own decisions while still supposedly under absolute jurisdiction of his parents according to Holy Scripture. Now he has developed a general attitude of rebellion. He dislikes authority and rejects rules of school or city. The problem here is that the parents did not heed the principle of growth from dependence to independence.

The opposite problem is seen in the person who is never released from dependence. Decisions are nearly impossible for this individual because his whole life up until the time he is released from home has been determined for him. He is allowed no questioning why, no discussion or reasoning, just obedience to commands. Such an atmosphere provides no motivation to move from a childish position of dependence to a position of adult independence. The line is a narrow one and, consequently, difficult to find. The difficulty, however, renders the search no less necessary for Christian parents.

A fourth guideline is that **the developing of basic Christian convictions depends upon a cooperation between the church and the home.** A new wind is blowing in Christian education these days about the importance of the Christian family. A relationship between church and home forms the basis for passage through the chaotic, confused, materialistic, relativistic world in which we live. God's priority on family life cannot be ignored by his people nor can it be relegated to a secondary place in Christian education.

The developing of basic Christian convictions is dependent upon an understanding of Biblical principles. There are certain things which the Bible clearly condemns. There is no question, for example, on matters such as murder and adultery. There is, however, a questionable area which includes many amusements and habit patterns. Here it becomes essential to build into Christian young people an understanding of the Biblical principles of Christian life and behavior. There are many such principles but the following five are, in my opinion, among the most helpful and relevant for maturity in Christian life today.

Universal Principles of Christian Behavior

The first is the principle of *Body Control* and is enunciated by the Apostle Paul in I Corinthians 6:

> For instance, take the matter of eating. God has given us an appetite for food and stomachs to digest it. But that doesn't mean we should eat more than we need. Don't think of eating as important, because some day God will do away with both stomachs and food. But sexual sin is never right: our bodies were not made

for that, but for the Lord, and the Lord wants to fill our bodies with Himself.

And God is going to raise our bodies from the dead by His power just as He raised up the Lord Jesus Christ.

Don't you realize that your bodies are actually parts and members of Christ? So should I take part of Christ and join Him to an harlot? Never!

And don't you know that if a man joins himself to an harlot that she becomes a part of him and he becomes a part of her? For God tells in the Old Testament that in His sight the two become one person.

But if you give yourself to the Lord, you and Christ are joined together as one person.

That is why I say run from sex sin. Every other sinful thing a man does hurts someone else, but this is sinning against his own body.

Haven't you yet learned that your body is the home of the Holy Spirit God gave you, and that He lives within you? Your own body does not belong to you.

For God has bought you with a great price. So use every part of your body to give glory to God, because He owns it. (I Corinthians 6:13-20 *The Living Bible*).

The Biblical principle of body control properly understood could eliminate immediately half of the controversial questions about behavior. The Christian must honestly come to grips with the issue of the indwelling Christ. He must realize, "God lives in me; where I go God goes, and what I eat God eats, and what I read, God reads." Although Paul's emphasis in the Corinthian passage is on immorality and fornication, the general implication asserts that the Spirit of God controls the believer's entire life.

A second Biblical principle is the principle of *Self Edification*. First Corinthians, chapter 10, and verse 23 states, "All things are lawful for me, but all things are not expedient: all things are lawful for me, but all things edify not." The principle of self edification simply states that the Christian ought to be always doing those things, thinking those thoughts and going to those places which will build up his life and make him more like Jesus Christ. We are not faced today with the question of meat offered to idols, but Paul was and his conclusion is that a perfectly "legal" practice for Christians may be a detriment to the spiritual development of others. All things were lawful for Paul but not all things constantly built him up. There is a great temptation to concern ourselves only with negatives, that is, things which hurt or hinder the spiritual life. Paul would urge us, however, to go one step further and ask, "How does this **help** me as a Christian?"

A third principle is the principle of *Habit Freedom,* also found in I Corinthians 6:12 "All things are lawful unto me but all things are not expedient: all things are lawful for me but I will not be brought under the power of any." Paul emphasizes in these two places that for the Christian, there is no set of rules or laws. Unfortunately, many Christians who adhere firmly to salvation by grace want to somehow write a code of laws by which to live the Christian life. One cannot, in proper Biblical perspective, legislate Christian living. It is possible for a believer to be cold in his Christian life even in spite of some kind of legalistic morality.

The words, *Life-Testimony,* describe a fourth principle of Pauline ethics. Paul avoided meat offered to idols, not because there was anything spiritually wrong in eating such meat, but because he was concerned about what misunderstanding such eating might do to hinder the growth of weaker Christians. Paul accepted the responsibility to govern his own behavior in such a way that the less mature Christian would never be led astray by anything he might do (I Corinthians 8).

This principle applied conscientiously today can answer many questions constantly debated in evangelical circles. Questionable practices may not be harmful to the person directly involved, but may cause stumbling in the lives of those who make decisions on the basis of another's life. Some Christians may be able to enjoy an occasional drink of wine without any detriment to spiritual growth or fear of direct condemnation from Scripture. A young Christian debating the issue of abstinence, however, could be led to violate his own convictions or worse because of the example of his more mature brother in Christ. Paul would choose abstinence in such a situation as this because of the principle of life testimony.

A final principle is all comprehensive and can be called the principle of *Christ Preeminence*. It is enunciated in Colossians 1:18 and involves a recognition of the Lord-disciple relationship so essential to effective Christian service. The believer comes to the place at which he completely commits his life to Jesus Christ. He no longer makes his own decisions or extols his own "rights" as an individual. The crucified self daily follows the "not I but Christ" policy of living. At this point of spiritual growth the Christian sheds the false legalism surrounding holy living and conducts his life in accordance with Biblical principles.

9

Sex Education in the Home

Little Jimmy jumped up on Dad's lap one evening and raised a question which Dad had been dreading for several years, "Dad, where did I come from?"

Folding aside his newspaper with great dignity, Dad mustered all his courage and prepared for a proper tonsorial rendering of his lecture on the birds and the bees. One hour later Jimmy yawned and said, "Sure Dad, I know all of that. But where did I come from? Billy came from Cincinnati, but where did **I** come from?"

In the Christian home parents should be concerned about attitude **toward** rather than facts **about.** To put it another way, in sex education more truth is caught than taught. Few educators, secular or Christian, would challenge the home as the central place for sex education because of the constant presence of object lessons and the possibility of the most conducive atmosphere for developing proper attitudes. Note that I have said that the home is the **best** place for sex education to take place. I did not say that most homes are doing the job, nor that most parents have the emotional, biological, and psychological equipment to undertake the task.

In the late 60s and early 70s the attention of Christian parents has been focused on sex education because of the development of programs of this type in public school systems. In January of 1968 Marjorie Iseman wrote in *McCalls,* "It's too late to debate whether there should be sex education in the schools. It's here. Schools have not merely accepted sex; they have embraced it". Some estimates suggest that 70% of the nation's schools already have broad, thorough sex education programs of one type or another. In short, sex education became in the late 60s what the removal of Bible reading and prayer from public schools was in the early and middle 60s—a catalyst for discussion and possible action on the part of Christian parents, evangelical churches, and Christian elementary and secondary schools.

It is my contention that tossing out a glib reference to the inadequacy of most parents to provide sex education, and then authorizing the presentation of that information by other sources is a "cop out". We all agree that at present most Christian homes are not equipped to face this position. But they can be, they should be, and it is the task of the church to provide them with the proper tools for the job.

Problems in Sex Education

Every youngster will obtain sex education. It may be correct, or it may be incorrect. It may be in the classroom, or it may be in the locker room. It may be in Christian books, or it may be in graffitti on restroom walls. But never-the-less, some attitude is developed and some information is gathered. In most cases parents attacking the problem of sex education discover that before they can communicate positive information, they must overcome the negative barriers which stand in the way. These barriers exist not only in the form of perverted viewpoints but also in various other accompanying problems which fog the air with respect to sex in general, and sex education in particular.

1. Fantasy Developed in the Mind of the Child

Children early become passive victims of improper conduct and verbalization on the part of the people around them. Too often those "people" include the parents themselves. In an issue of *Family Life,* Popenoe talks about myths in sex education and says,

Much sex education has been unsatisfactory because of the lack of correct information on the part of those teaching it. The whole subject has long been cluttered up with superstitions, half-truths, and gross errors, many of which are found in publications that are supposed to be from competent sources.[1]

Although these fantasies may be developed in the mind while a child, they continue on through teen years and even come back to haunt adults and disrupt otherwise happy marriages.

2. Gutter Education With Its Raw Facts and Perverted Attitude

A biology of restroom walls is available very early to the children and young people in our society. On the basis of this perverted information and the grossly distorted information of classmates and neighborly friends, they construct a very "low brow" opinion of their own sexuality and the role of sex in society. A proper concept of sex must begin with a Biblical view of the roles of husbands and wives in the home.   That is never learned in the street, and often not learned in formal sex education experiences.

3. Ignorance and Fear on Part of the Parents

Jesus once told a group of Saducees, "Ye do err not knowing the scriptures" (Matthew 22:29). This ignorance and fear rather represents a cause-effect relationship with respect to the solving of problems.

(1) The parents themselves had inadequate sex education. In a *Moody Monthly* article Wayne Christianson quotes the comment of a Christian father:

When we were married, both my wife and I felt that we were fairly well informed. Actually, we knew much less than we thought. We knew about the obvious things and virtually nothing about the things that really matter — the place of love, our importance to one an-

1. Paul Popenoe, "Some Myths in Sex Education", *Family Life*, Vol. XXIX, No. 2, Feb. 1969, p. 1.

other and the niche sex comes to have in healthy Christian lives. We've learned most of these things, I guess, but many of them came the hard way — and ten to twenty years too late.[2]

(2) The relationship between many parents is a poor model for their children. In saying "more is caught than taught" one recognizes that what children see their parents do and hear their parents say becomes more important in framing permanent attitudes toward sex than those things which their parents tell them about sexuality. The father who spends some of his time shouting at his wife is demonstrating a poor sample for his young daughter who may thereby develop a fear of marriage; or for his young son who may conclude that manhood is gauged by the volume of one's anger. Verbal concern about the excesses of *SIECUS* is a fraud unless Christian parents are undertaking to develop and control a home for the purpose of positive, Christian sex education. Children must see positive examples of proper conduct to offset the rank barbarianism of Hollywood and the other mass media.

(3) Parents tend to possess Victorian ideas and fears about sex. There is, of course, a major difference between Victorian ideas and the ideas of the Bible. When one condemns "Victorian ideas" some readers will think that this is a thrust for the new morality and a condemnation of anything that is old. As a matter of fact, it is rather an appeal for something that is considerably older than the distorted and perverted cultural theology of Victorianism in England and Puritanism in America. The difference between the view of sex defined in the Bible and those of Victorianism and Puritanism is (in the case of adultery) the difference between the forgiveness of Christ for the woman in John chapter 8 and the branding of Hester Prynne in Nathaniel Hawthorne's novel, *The Scarlet Letter*.

2. Wayne Christianson, "Must the Church Be Silent on Sex"?, *Moody Monthly,* Jan. 1968, p. 18.

4. Failure of the Church to Provide Equipment for the Task

Of what does this equipment consist? Perhaps that question would be answered differently by different churches and cultural areas of North America, as well as the world. At least three things come to focus, however; a stimulus or motivation to parents to undertake the job of sex education in the home; clear cut instruction in Biblical views of sex and how such information can be built into the nurture program; and a careful delineation of the spiritual and biblical foundations for human sexuality. From the *Moody Monthly* article mentioned above, I quote Robert R. Murfin, Executive Director of the Evangelical Child Welfare Agency in Chicago, "If the Christian family cannot give answers to its teen-agers and the average family cannot, the family will lose them to someone who can. If the church in turn is silent, the church will lose them too . . ."[3]

Opportunities for Sex Education in The Home

One of the features which makes the home such a viable context for sex education is the frequent happening of events which provide a significant stimulus for good sex education. The following list of eight is hardly exhaustive, but it does provide a suggested list which can give Christian parents some idea of when informal nurture can take place in the teaching of Biblical sexuality.

1. A New Baby in the Home or Neighborhood

As a pregnancy becomes obvious it is natural for children in the family to ask questions. How foolish are the answers given by many Christian parents in their attempts to avoid the subject, when all they need to say is, "God is making a baby grow inside of mother." The enthusiasm with which mom and dad await the arrival of the new baby, and their verbalizations of what is happening, provide at least a six month course in sex education with attitudes being formed every day.

---

3. loc. cit.

Common terminology such as "labor pains" may even prejudice a little girl negatively toward the experience she anticipates in the future. Some Christian psychologists suggest that children be allowed to observe breast feeding while having explained to them precisely how God ordained this form of physical nurture. The imagery in Scripture may be used to talk about spiritual nurture.

2. Observing Parents or Other Children Bathing, Toileting, etc.

If junior takes a shower with dad he will very quickly ask the meaning of parts of the male body and how they are different from the bodily parts of little sister and mommy. There are perfectly good answers for such questions and no Christian father should be embarrassed to give them, and give them accurately.

3. Care of Pets

Why does the dog need to be penned up when she is in heat? What about the process of the delivery of that calf? Why do rabbits have so many babies? Every question is a beautiful opportunity for the explanation of not only animalistic biological fact, but the parallel explanation of the growth of the family in love.

4. When Children Use Sex Words

Sometimes such a word may have no meaning at all for the child. He just heard the boys on the street use it, and so he used it at home. Rather than rushing for the soap to administer just punishment for such "dirty talk", the parent should view this as a golden opportunity to explain the word and the proper context for its use. The administration of the soap may extinguish all further uses of the word, but it also might extinguish any willingness to discuss words and concepts of a similar nature with parents.

5. After Attending A Wedding

Christian weddings are full of symbolism. Just like many of the feasts in the Old Testament, the symbolism can be used as an educational catalyist. Why is white always used in a wedding? Why does the groom kiss the bride only once in the ceremony, and why does he do it in front of all those people? Why do brides and grooms exchange rings at the wedding? Why did the bride carry a Bible? Why do people give gifts? How much more significant a motivator for education is the wedding than the classroom!

6. Observing His Own Body

Totally apart from seeing the anatomy of other persons, the child will soon raise questions about his own body. Sometimes his observation is physical rather than verbal as parents notice him playing with parts of the body. Rather than slapping hands and building in a negative disposition toward sex organs, the parents can explain why it is improper to engage in that sort of behavior, and how God has ordained a significant use for the sex organs.

7. Mass Media and Books

Almost all children watch television. Even in Christian homes where the controls on what is watched may be carefully exercised, there will be ample opportunity in the most innocent and wholesome of programs for children to observe behavior and incidents which can and will trigger questions about sex. There is no point in trying to keep the child away from all such influences. Parents should recognize in them what professional educators call "teachable moments" and be ready to capture them for the purposes of Christian nurture.

8. Formal Instructional Times

Probably 90% of all the child learns about sex will take place in informal questions and situations such as those described above. There ought to be, however, a definite effort on the part of the parents to program into the life of the home, periods of sex education which are deliberately constructed for that purpose. These need not be classroom sessions in which a child sits and listens to a lecture nervously delivered by one of the parents. Perhaps they will consist of deliberately planned conversations between father and son or mother and daughter; the showing of filmstrips such as those produced in conjunction with the Concordia Sex Education series; the reading and discussion of literature written for children and young people on the subject of Christian education (see bibliography); and attending formal sex education classes in church or Christian school.

Principles for Christian Sex Education

There is no principle more significant than the emphasis made by Clair Amstutz that Biblical love must be the cradle for sex education if the baby is going to grow up healthy and normal.[4] Christian love is a clearly defined Biblical attitude and not an emotion. It is considerably more than the definition which someone has offered, "an inward inexpressability of an outward alloverishness". Once that context has been clearly formulated, then the rest of the task becomes relatively easy providing the Christian keeps himself informed and observes some guide lines for sex education in the home. To keep the principles parallel with the opportunities, here are eight simple guide lines for accomplishing the task:

1. Always Encourage Open Communication in the Home

Don't slap mouths, don't censure statements, don't inhibit the child's natural expression of his thoughts to his parents. Obviously we are not advocating here a continual receptivity to the behavior of children when that behavior has been expressly condemned over a period of time. The focus here is on spontaneous outbursts of sexual words, phrases or ideas which children will emit from time to time.

2. Answer All Questions Directly, Honestly, and Simply

Do not provide more information than that for which the child has asked. One of the myths of sex education

---

4. H. Clair Amstutz, *Growing Up To Love,* Scottdale, Pennsylvania: Herald Press, 1956.

is that fathers should always answer the questions that boys ask and mothers should always answer the questions that girls ask. Actually both parents should be willing to answer either child because each parent is the parent of all his children. As the children grow older they will tend to gravitate toward the parent of the same sex with their questions. In the early days, however, the children should get the impression that sex is an open subject in the family and that either parent can speak with authority on the issues.

3. Always Exercise Positive Parental Example

Rather than shouting at each other affection should be seen between parents, the enjoyment of being close, embracing frequently, and impressing the observing children that tenderness and warmth go hand in hand in the relationship between husband and wife. Children who observe this normal behavior frequently in the home will not be embarrassed when they see it and will tend to accept it and emulate it as the natural course of events in the Christian home, which of course, it should be.

4. Teach Sex Positively, Not Negatively

Children and young people should look forward with pleasure to marriage, child bearing, and the other sexual aspects of parenthood. The mother whose unhappy marital experience causes her to say to her daughter, "you can never trust a man", is leading her daughter to the very unfortunate experiences she would like her to avoid. The dad who is observed by his young son reading *Playboy* may discover that his son develops a philosophy in which he thinks of women as property rather than people.

5. Be Spiritual and Biblical Throughout

Children should understand the *why* of Christian marriage not only the *what* and the *how*. Sex education is meaningless unless it is based on the principle that marriage exists primarily for fellowship between the husband and the wife which is parallel to the communion between Christ and his church.

6. Be Casual and Informal

Sex is a natural and common part of living. It only takes on grotesque and unnatural forms when we superimpose those forms upon it. Sex education should not be stimulating to older children and teens, but rather just as normal as learning other kinds of behavior patterns essential to life. Furthermore, the proper response of the sexes to each other is a genuine pleasure and it doesn't have to be treated in a sanctimonious, hyper-Puritanism which locks its secrets in a golden box. Such an attitude too often discovers that the box turns out to be Pandora's.

7. Use Scientific Terms for the Parts of the Body

Parents who propogate myths about child birth or make up strange and meaningless names for parts of the body will soon discover that a credibility gap develops with respect to sex education and the confidence which children have in the parent's authority to speak on the subject. Only perverted people say that sex is basically wrong. How foolish to adopt this strange nomenclature for parts of the body when accurate terminology does exist. By what strange contortion of truth are these words thought to be spiritual?

8. Base Your Biology on Sound Christian Theology

The sovereignty of God and the Lordship of Jesus Christ are foundation stones for a proper view of God's order in the family. The Biblical concepts of absolute truth and a celestial value system preempt the relative truth and situation ethics which dominate much of public sex education in the 1970s. Any education which does not recognize the fact that all men are the creation of the sovereign self-revealed God must eventually distort a truthful view of sex education at best, and turn it into nothing more than animal biology at worst. Such errors should never be propagated in the Christian home and do not have to be if the evangelical church will shoulder its responsibility in ministering to the whole man and therefore provide programs in Biblical sex education for its people.

Sex Education Bibliography
(For Parents)

Amstutz, H. Clair. *Growing Up to Love*. Scottdale, Pennsylvania: Herald Press, 1956.

Baruch, Dorothy, *New Ways in Sex Education*. New York: McGraw - Hill, 1959.

Greenblat, Bernard R. *A Doctor's Marital Guide for Patients*. Chicago: Budlong Press, 1957.

Kolb, Erwin J. *Parents Guide to Christian Conversation About Sex*. St. Louis: Concordia Publishing House, 1967.

Lewin, Samuel A. and John Gilmore. *Sex Wtihout Fear*. New York: Medical Research Press, 1951.

Narramore, Clyde. *How to Tell Your Children About Sex*. Grand Rapids: Zondervan Publishing House, 1958.

Rice, Termon B. *Those First Sex Questions*. American Medical Association.

Wessler, Martin F. *Christian View of Sex Education*. St. Louis Concordia Publishing House, 1967.

When Children Ask About Sex. Child Study Association of America, New York, 1953.

Sex Education Bibliography
(For Children and Young People)

Bueltmann, A. J. *Take the High Road*. St. Louis: Concordia Publishing House, 1967. (Jr. High).

Duvall, Evelyn and Sylvanus Duvall. *Sex Ways in Fact and Faith; Basis for Christian Family Policy*. New York: Association Press, 1961.

Frey, Marguerite Kay. *I Wonder, I Wonder*. St. Louis: Concordia Publishing House, 1967. (Preschoolers and Primaries).

Gruenberg, S. M. *The Wonderful Story of How You Were Born*. Hanover House, 1953. (Primaries).

Hummel, Ruth. *Wonderfully Made*. St. Louis: Concordia Publishing House, 1967. (Juniors).

Richards, Larry, *How Far Can I Go?* Chicago: Moody Press, 1969. (Teens).

Scahzoni, Letha. *Sex and the Single Eye*. Grand Rapids: Zondervan Publishing House, 1968 (Teens).

Trobisch, Walter. *I Loved A Girl*. New York: Harper and Row, 1965. (Teens).

Witt, Homer. *Life Can Be Sexual*. St. Louis: Concordia Publishing House, 1967. (Teens).

10

Avoiding Divorce: Legal and Practical

In 1969 the National Center for Statistics reported that the United States had a higher divorce rate since 1962 than any other country for which information was reported to the statistical office of the United Nations. Egypt ranks number two, countries of the Communist block follow, then Scandinavian and other European countries, with Japan in the thirteenth spot. The divorce rate for the United States is generally considered to be about one out of every three marriages or to calculate it another way, 2.5 divorces granted per one thousand population. The March 1970 issue of *Family Life* carried a table showing almost 4 divorces per one thousand population in 10 out of the fifty states.[1]

Actually, listing a divorce rate in relationship to the state population is somewhat deceiving since divorce rates are often calculated in this manner by declaring the ratio between the number of marriages and divorces in the same year. In this situation the number of marriages around the state tends to make the impact of the divorce rate lower. The American Institute of Family Relations argues almost all statistics are conservative and that the divorce rate is indeed "increasing in recent years, and this increase cannot be explained by the growth in the number of young married couples."[2] In

1. *Family Life,* March 1970, Vol. 30, No. 3, p. 1,2.
2. Ibid, p. 3.

reference to the last matter a recent survey shows that almost 20% of husbands and 50% of the wives divorced in 1965 were married in their teens.[3]

A motivating factor in the *increasing* divorce rate is the *decreasing* seriousness of attitude with which Western Society views the disintegration of marriage. Mostly the effect is general apathy but sometimes radicalism asserts its ugly head. For example a Unitarian minister operating in Virginia has prepared a dignified ten minute service "for couples who want to dissolve their marriages with the comfort, concern, and blessing of the church". The introductory paragraph of his ceremony ends with the line, "we have come to witness and participate in a solemn and awesome act: a rite of divorce".[4] Even Christians have had their Biblical senses dulled by the songs of the secularized society which not only affirm the validity of divorce but actually proclaim its desirability in many marital situations.

What is The Biblical View of Divorce?

As nearly as I can determine, there are three rather common positions with respect to what the Bible has to say about divorce.

1. There are Various Reasons for Divorce

This would be a position primarily held by secular marriage counselors and by many liberal clergymen. Very few evangelicals would even pay lip service to this point of view since it is so obviously contradictory to the teaching of both Old and New Testament. A willingness to go to war over any issue demonstrates a country's insincerity when it speaks about peace. In the same way, a willingness to talk freely about the validity of divorce shows a person's insincerity with respect to the sanctity and permanency of the family bond.

2. There is One Biblical Reason for Divorce

Perhaps this position is the one most commonly held

---

3. Divorce Statistics Analysis, 1964 and 1965, National Center for Health Statistics Series 21, No. 17, October 1969.
4. *Newsweek,* October 24, 1966, p. 105.

among evangelical Christian leaders. The "one Biblical reason" would be defined as adultery and persons holding this position would draw their arguments from Matthew five and similar passages. Frequently the words "innocent party" are used to describe the person who was wronged by his or her marriage partner's infidelity.

3. There is No Biblical Reason for Divorce

Everybody is a member of some minority group and persons holding this position soon discover that they are a remnant people. The position is based upon a distinction between the acts of fornication and adultery and the use of these words in the scripture. Adultery is described as "marital unchastity" whereas fornication is defined as "premarital unchastity". The arguments suggest that the Bible allows a formal "divorce" in cases of fornication but never in cases of adultery. To put it another way, the Bible allows persons who are not married to be divorced, but never persons who are married.

If this sounds like so much nonsense it might be important to add that Jewish culture observed in both the Old and New Testaments demonstrates vigorous laws controlling the state of engagement. There is a good illustration of this in the case of the earthly parents of our Lord. *Before* the wedding Joseph thought that he had discovered his bride-to-be was pregnant. The scripture tells us that he did not want to make a public example of her and so he was going to privately put her away. In actuality the law called for him to write a bill of divorcement and legally declare her to be guilty of fornication and therefore unfit for the pending marriage. Remember that the Old Testament prescription for adultery (marital unchastity) was not divorce, but rather death by stoning! Advocates of position three usually emphasize a passage in Romans at the beginning of chapter seven in which Paul tells the believers that a woman is bound to her husband "as long as he liveth" and is not released by any piece of paper issued by an earthly court.

I have detailed the third position to a greater extent not because I wish to "shove it down the reader's theological throat", but because it has not received wide hearing in evangelical circles and deserves at least a modicum of attention in the pages of this treatment of the subject.

Some Related Questions

There are numerous questions which rush to the fore when one deals with this threatened shipwreck on the sea of matrimony called "divorce". Presuming that the initial question concerning Biblical views has been satisfactorily settled, one then has to ask, "Can a divorced person remarry? And if so under what circumstances?" Here again positions held by genuine evangelicals differ widely. Many would say that the "innocent party" has no Biblical limitations to his or her second marriage. Others suggest that only under certain circumstances can a person be wed again within the blessing of God. Others who espouse the position of "no Biblical reason for divorce" would argue that even when a person has been passively divorced by another (and has not contested the proceedings) he is still not free to remarry.

Remarriage is, as the British would say, "a sticky wicket". Statistics show that a much higher percentage of second marriages end in divorce so we are right to wonder whether "love is more beautiful the second time around". In actuality a recent survey by the University of Toronto Bureau of Social Work shows that after divorce, the majority of persons marry usually within a few years, for the second time.[5] Second marriage is a risky business and Christians must give themselves carefully to serious personal Bible study and prayer before a decision is reached on such a question.

Another difficult question which clamors for attention raises the issue of whether a Christian minister should marry a person who has been divorced? The answer obviously is a relative one. That is, it is related

---

5. Benjamin Schlisinger, "Success for Remarriage after Divorce", *Family Life,* January, 1969, Vol. XXIX, No. 1.

to one's initial position on divorce. If one believes that
there is no Biblical reason for divorce, he would consequently believe that remarrying a divorced person
would be assisting that person to commit adultery. On
the other hand, if one believes that there are some legitimate reasons for divorce, he might conclude that the
"innocent party" has every right to another wedding
with sanction of the church.

What is the proper Biblical role if a person's unsaved
partner seeks divorce? For the answer to this question
we must turn to I Corinthians chapter seven.

> "And unto the married I command, yet not I,
> but the Lord, let not the wife depart from her
> husband: But and if she depart, let her remain
> unmarried, or be reconciled to her husband:
> and let not the husband put away his wife. But
> to the rest speak I, not the Lord: If any brother
> hath a wife that believeth not, and she be
> pleased to dwell with him, let him not put her
> away. And the woman which hath an husband
> that believeth not, and if he be pleased to
> dwell with her, let her not leave him. For the
> unbelieving husband is sanctified by the wife,
> and the unbelieving wife is sanctified by the
> husband: else were your children unclean; but
> now are they holy. But if the unbelieving de-
> part, let him depart. A brother or a sister is not
> under bondage in such cases: But God hath
> called us to peace. For what knowest thou, O
> wife, whether thou shalt save thy husband?
> Or how knowest thou, O man, whether thou
> shalt save thy wife?"

The conclusion which we draw from this passage is
that it is proper for the Christian to allow his or her
spouse to depart if that is the wish of the unsaved
partner. On the other hand, if the unsaved partner is
willing to live with the Christian, the latter should not
seek a divorce on the basis that they are not both
members of the family of God. This passage may refer
only to a specific situation at a specific point in time.

On the other hand it may very well be laying a general principle for all marriages at all times.

Issues Which Lead to Divorce

In the above paragraphs we have been talking about legal divorce. Statistics show that Christian families have very little threat of legal divorce. Experience shows, however, that they live in more significant danger of what I am choosing to call "practical divorce". This terminology is used to describe a family situation in which husband and wife would never go to the courts regardless of how intolerable the situation might become. Fear of public opinion, commitment to a church position, or genuine concern for Biblical values would force them to hold the union together whatever the cost.

Meanwhile they are living in a state of constant "practical divorce" by existing together under the same roof but in a house made empty by the absence of love, dependence, and warm human relationships. They have probably also long since stopped sleeping together and the home has become a role situation in which family members rest and refuel. Obviously this position is not glorifying to God and represents a deterioration of all qualities of those persons; spiritual, and emotional as well as physical and mental. One of the purposes of books like this is to help Christian families stay out of the path that leads to "practical divorce". Remember that a happy family is not one without problems but one that handles its difficulties with understanding and love. Consider the following examples of marital disagreements:

1. Disagreements Over the Relationship to In-laws

Too many marriages have suffered weakness because a wife or husband was not able to sever his or her ties with parents. The establishment of the newly founded family both Biblically and sociologically requires a certain "break" with previous parental advice-giving and control.

2. Disagreements Over Money and Budget

On a survey of marriages in the Detroit area, Robert Blood and Donald Wolfe asked wives the question, "Since you were married, what are the things you and your husband have disagreed about?" Twenty-four percent of those tabulated indicated that money was the chief disagreement and 42% listed it in the category of "total disagreement". The researchers concluded that "financial problems pop up in more marriages than any other category of disagreement".[6]

3. Disagreements Over Child Discipline

This was the second most frequently listed item in the Blood and Wolfe survey. One reason why this issue becomes a contentious one is because husbands and wives do not take enough time to discuss proper methodology for the discipline of children and fail to maintain consistent standards for the behavior of children in the home.

4. Disagreements Over the Husband's Busy Schedule

There is no question about the fact that the pressure-cooker society in which we live makes the development of sound family structure most difficult. The man who must travel one hour each way to his business in the city besides spending eight or nine hours there, finds himself on the short end of the clock when it becomes necessary to spend some time with wife and children. But here again we are dealing with the matter of priorities. It is not so much a question of how the husband spends all his time, but rather *how he chooses to spend that time which he can afford to invest as he chooses.* Of course the Christian husband will be honest in determining how many of the hours in a week he can actually control for himself.

5. Disagreements Over the Wife's Care of the Home

Paul told Titus to teach the older women to teach the younger women to be keepers at home. The old adage, "a woman's place is in the home" does not stem

6. Robert O. Blood, Jr. and Donald M. Wolfe, *Husbands and Wives: The Dynamics of Married Living*, New York, The Free Press, p. 240, 241.

from a pre-scientific agrarian society, but rather from the teaching of the Word of God. Particularly if the husband has a neat secretary who keeps the office in shining order will the wife suffer by comparison if that man must come home to a sloppy, disheveled mess.

6. Disagreement Over Activities Outside the Home

Who will be our friends? What families will we visit frequently? Should the husband have a night off to himself for bowling or "a night with the boys?" Should the wife have an opportunity to spend time apart from her husband with her "girlfriends?" These and other questions like them must be carefully answered by mutual consent before they erupt into divisive quarrels in the Christian home.

7. Disagreements Arising from Educational Differences

So far as it is possible, the wife ought to reach *toward* the academic attainments of her husband. That does not mean that the man who has an earned doctorate must have a wife with a similar degree in order to insure a happy home. It does mean, however, that the man who has attained a high level of education will find himself increasingly intellectually separated from his wife if she makes no effort through reading, asking questions, and generally involving herself in his field, to keep up with him as a thinking equal. Of course if wives are to learn from their husbands at home as Paul indicated, there is a responsibility for the husband to share with his wife those things which he finds intellectually stimulating. Incidentally this is a good argument against young ladies dropping out of college to support their husbands while they finish. A Ph.T. (Putting Hubby Through) degree may be nobly earned but when it comes to intellectual conversation 5 or 6 years later it will not compare with the Bachelor's or Master's degree it may have replaced.

8. Disagreements Over Conflicting Tastes

This is a broad category dealing with everything from the type of clothes worn by one's mate to disturbing quirks of personality. One would think that these types of things had been taken care of back in the dating stage but sometimes they don't show up until after marriage and perhaps are even developed later in life. The success of a happy home depends not on avoiding all these issues because they will arise, but rather on talking and praying through the conflict so that agreement arises out of disagreement.

Dr. Henry Brandt draws upon the generally approved procedures of problem-solving to suggest a format for the amelioration of conflicts in marriage.

(1) Identify and isolate the problem, the *real* problem.

(2) Gather information (facts) which help to arrive at a solution.

(3) List possible solutions, possibly through the process of brain storming.

(4) Evaluate the possible solutions.

(5) Select the solution which seems best.

(6) Implement the decision and stick with it.

(7) Permeate the whole process with the proper attitude, a submission to the will of God; a submission to the Word of God, mutual dependence on prayer, and an open-mindedness and willingness to compromise.

11

Parents, Pastors, and Premarital Counseling

The implications of the title of this chapter cannot be mistaken. I am taking the position that a young person's parents **and** his pastor are responsible for preparing him for marriage and the development of the Christian home. This is not primarily a task for trained specialists for as Carl Rogers says, "the gigantic need makes any foreseeable increase in specialists merely 'a study in futility'." Rogers chooses the broad view dealing with the counseling of married persons; whereas this chapter deals only with **pre**marital counseling. But the degree of need and the availability of means to meet it are not appreciably different. Specialists alone cannot meet either one.

Appreciating the Necessity
For Premarital Counseling

Marriage is serious and sacred business. It has always been that and always will be but because of the increasingly secularized context of society, Christians must call more loudly and clearly than ever for a careful program of preparation for marriage. The church is important to young families but young families are also important to the church. Apart from the ministry of the local church and the strategic nature of the gathered body of Christ as a corporeal representation of the Savior on earth, there is a vacuum of Biblical information which makes it imperative that we draw families to the church even before they become families.

Obviously a thorough program of premarital instruction will include more than a few sessions with the pastor as Westberg clearly emphasizes:

> When ministers began to do premarital counseling they were the target for friendly kidding about "how to make a happy marriage in three easy lessons". We entertain no illusions as to what can be accomplished by a few talks with the minister. Perhaps the great contribution this movement has made is to call attention to the many ways in which local churches can contribute to education for Christian marriage long before the wedding is in sight. Premarital counseling has pointed up the seriousness of marriage and has discouraged couples from assuming they could enter into it lightly. It has also encouraged a continuing discussion after the marriage ceremony of ways to face daily problems in accord with Christian principles.

> Young people seem particularly proud to be able to say that "our church doesn't marry people until they have taken a course of instruction." As a result, engaged couples whose wedding date is many months away call the church office to ask when they are supposed to begin their "lessons". These couples are sincere in their desire to have their marriage get off to a good start and are willing to go quite out of their way to make preparations for it.

Another part of the problem is the apparent unwillingness of many pastors to engage in serious preparation of their young people for marriage. Not only do they not structure a formal program of instruction, but the counseling session itself often consists of nothing more than an attempt to establish that both members of the proposed union are genuine Christians.

Establishing a Climate for Premarital Counseling

The pastor who is genuinely desirous of establishing a climate for premarital counseling will be preaching and teaching regularly on the subject of the Christian home. His church will probably have at least one Family Life Conference (perhaps a weekend in early Spring) per year and his position on the subjects of marriage and divorce will be well known to his parishioners. He is a friend and a confidant of persons of all ages in his congregation. He is approachable and his office is accessible to teen-agers. Young people who have had very little contact with their pastor for twenty years will not feel comfortable in the intimate sessions of premarital counseling. He will be ready to help them as much as he can.

If the tone for family life education has been set through pulpit ministry and informal conversation through the years, the specific task of counseling and instruction for marriage will be made much easier. Now the church already knows the pastor's stand on divorce, remarriage, birth control, abortion, and other factors which relate to family life education. When such a climate of acceptance and mutual trust has been established, the pastor is in a good position to require a formal program of premarital counseling and instruction before he agrees to perform a wedding.

Developing a Program of Premarital Counseling

The purpose of premarital counseling is to help people come to marriage with a mature and proper perspective. It also serves the purpose of leading Christian young people to prepare for a Christ-honoring ceremony in their marriage. The pastor who successfully carries on a program of premarital counseling and instruction can thereby establish pastoral or counselor rapport for the handling of family problems. The successful adjustment of the counselees in their relationship to each other and the establishment of a Christian home are facilitated by the successful counseling process. Just like any other educational endeavor, premarital instruction and counseling need to have clear-cut objectives if they are to accomplish a clear-cut goal.

Counseling During the Dating Period

Along with the regular preaching and teaching ministry described above, counseling during the dating period will be mostly passive or "nondirective" in nature. This is a crucial time, however, and pastors and parents will want to do some very positive and concrete things during these late teen years.

1. Provide A Healthy Social Atmosphere For Teenagers and Encourage Wholesome Christian Companionship

The church has no option regarding the gregarious relationship nature of youth activities. The only choice is whether it will provide opportunities for companionship in which it serves as host and guide, rather than abandoning its youth to the secularized and over-sexed activity of a pagan society.

2. Provide Sound Scriptural Preaching On Christian Home and Family Living

The content of premarital counseling should be no shock to the young couple who have been in attendance at the church's educational activities through the years.

3. Provide Directive Teaching In Sunday School During the Dating Years

If we really wish our teaching to be life-related (and all Christian Educators pay lip service at this altar), then we need to deal with those issues which are a part of life at different times in the human experience of the individual. This is sometimes referred to as "developmental task education". The successful experience of the first date and the continuing dating relationship is certainly a developmental task. The selection of a life mate and a decision to enter a period of "engagement" is also a significant developmental task.

4. Provide Guided Activities In Evening Youth Groups

The traditional Sunday evening activity for young

people is called "training hour". Its characteristic is a focus on experiential involvement in the kind of situations which youth will face as adult leaders. Certainly the most pressing role which they face is that of father or mother, so obviously we ought to structure panel discussions, films, special speakers, and study groups which center in family life education.

5. Provide Private Interviews With Pastors and Christian Leaders

A competent adult counselor should meet with teenagers in church at least once a year. This kind of program does not have to be forced and stiff but could center more on what Howard Hendricks has often called "Coca Cola Counseling".

6. Provide Literature Carefully Selected and Attractively Presented

There has never been a day in which Christians have had a greater supply of literature aimed at both adults and teens on the subject of marriage and family. We need to get our youth reading things like *I Loved A Girl* and *The Teen-ager You're Dating*. The bibliography at the end of the previous chapter contains several suggested items.

Counseling During Engagement

The engagement period is taken too lightly by many Christian leaders. It is often considered a cultural nicety at best, and a waste of time at worst. In actuality it is an extremely crucial part of a successful preparation for marriage. The American Institute of Family Relations reports that 40% of the *unhappily* married persons who come to its office for help admit that they had no engagement period whatever! In many cases marriage was an impulsive, spur-of-the-moment act. Popenoe not only emphasizes the importance of engagements but lends his considerable influence to a relatively long engagement period.

> Our studies of hundreds of marriages show
> that the average couple know each other for
> two or three years, and have been definitely

engaged for about a year before they marry. The studies of E. W. Burgess and L. S. Cottrell Jr., at the University of Chicago, fully confirm the extensive experience of the American Institute of Family Relations. Summed up succinctly, this is what they reveal.

Beyond all doubt, the happiest marriages are those in which the partners have known each other for several years before their proposal and have been engaged for some months before a wedding.

The actual structure of the counseling interviews can be individually determined by the pastor who is carrying them out. Several principles, however, seem to characterize successful premarital counseling programs. One is that the interviews are stretched out over a period of time, sometimes as much as four to six weeks. Another characteristic is that the counseling program is supplemented by specific reading assignments which expose the young people to the best literature available. A third common quality of good premarital counseling programs is the willingness of many pastors to bring in other professional personalities such as a Christian doctor or a Christian psychologist.

Such programs cover a broad area of categories but put heavy emphasis on the Christian interpretation of love and marital relations. The course includes sex relations but does not push the physical side of marriage out of proper proportion. Good premarital counseling also focuses on the cultivation and maturation of love, the negative and positive aspects of parenthood, and the physical, emotional and psychological adjustment of marriage partners.

At least one interview needs to be given to planning the ceremony itself. It should be a genuine testimony to all who attend. But before it can be that, the young couple needs to understand the meaning of a marriage ceremony. Detailed planning will take in such factors as date, place, time, personnel, location of the reception, seating, music, etc.

Many pastors also like to have a a post-ceremony interview during which they dedicate the home to Christ and discuss some of the practical implementation of things which may have been theory two months before. This interview can deepen the interest for the couple in the program of the church and perhaps enlist them for some form of Christian service. Obviously this interview is best held at the married couple's home, rather than in the pastor's office. Periodic visits to the home during the first year offer more help in handling the important issues clarified during the sessions of premarital instruction and counseling.

But the responsibility for premarital counseling does not rest on the pastor alone. That is precisely correct. Although he may be the professional with respect to preparation for marriage and the theological implications of home and family life, he does not bear the ultimate responsibility for what happens to the young people whose weddings he performs. That is the direct concern of their parents. Consequently, parents ought to involve themselves in premarital counseling even though that may be on a much less formal plane than the sessions directed by the pastor. Furthermore, that counseling does not begin two months before the wedding but actually emerges as soon as the young teen-ager is able to think of himself in a familial role. If parents are doing their job properly the formal counseling sessions offered by the pastor just before the wedding will be merely "a confirmation" of what the young people have long since learned at home.

Perhaps a word to pastors would be in order with respect to the example of the pastor's family. The home life which has been on exhibit for the church's young people to see while they are growing up now forms the frame of reference out of which any pastoral counseling sessions emerge. Does the young person want his home to be like the home of his pastor? Would he like to have his wife react to him the way the pastor's wife behaves the times he has watched her? Does the young lady hope that her new husband will treat her the way the pastor treats his wife? As Narramore has said, "It makes no difference how many doctorate degrees you have or how beautifully you can speak, what great insights or intellect you might have — it is what you are at home that counts. The reflection of your home life goes with you into the pulpit. You may seem to get by for awhile living one kind of life at home and another in the pulpit but it will eventually end in defeat". Certainly what is said here about the pulpit ministry is also true in the counseling ministry.

Sometimes the best kind of premarital counseling will be negative. That is, pastors and parents will try to discourage the young couple from going ahead with the wedding, at least at this time. Such an honest confrontation with reality may not always produce a happy reaction on the part of the anticipating lovers but it may well be within the realm of proper and mature leadership on the part of that pastor or those parents. There are simply some young people who should not marry each other and there are others who should wait for another year or two before entering into this most serious business of establishing a Christian home.

Footnotes

1. Granger Westberg, Premarital Counseling Department of Family Life National Council of Churches of Christ in U.S.A. New York, New York, 1958, p. 6.
2. *The American Institute of Family Relations,* Publication No. 18, "Those Engagement Revelations", p. 1.

12

Church and Home: Conflict, Compromise, or Cooperation?

In December 1970, conferees at the White House Conference on Children issued a major report warning that "America's families are in trouble— trouble so deep and pervasive as to threaten the future of our nation." California psychologist Richard Farson told the delegates that the family as we presently know it is often without function and is no longer necessarily the basic unit in our society. Dr. Paul Popenoe of the American Institute of Family Relations uttered an ominous note: "No society has ever survived after its family life deteriorated."

One's view on the gravity of the situation may vary in intensity but most experts agree that life in the American family is facing a decade of danger which is perhaps unparalleled in the history of the world since the time of Christ.

It would seem that Christian families could turn to their churches in such a time of crisis, but can they? Is the local church of the 1970s a help or a hindrance to the proper functioning of a Christian home? Certainly the pages of both the Old and New Testaments indicate that the family is of *first* importance. It existed before churches or synagogues and from the divine viewpoint, continues to the present hour as the primary institution of love and learning. In the Middle Ages ecclesiastical control over church life tended to stifle the dynamic of the individual home but Luther recaptured Biblical norms when he and Katie showed Germany what a godly home should look like.

Today we give our children to the public school for general education; to the church for religious education; to the Little League for recreation; to summer camp for a vacation; and to the babysitter for discipline. In spite of the fact that the subject of "family" occupies 30 pages in the Hitchcock Topical Bible, we tend to be swept along by the views of secular sociologists and psychologists into adopting the position that a home is a temporary pitstop on the racetrack of life.

Problems in Church-Home Relations

But many churches are reevaluating their programs and purposes in light of the Biblical emphasis on the home. Some of them are experiencing great discouragement. Several pastors have told me that it is impossible to make a genuine impact on family life today. So many other factors, organizations, and events clamor for attention that the church cannot be heard. Because of the difficulty, some have given up in their efforts to really achieve a balanced and mutually profitable relationship between the church and its homes. Other church leaders have not yet made the attempts at cooperation. They tend to disjoin the two institutions and view them as separate entities. They may admit the importance of both, but program their church activities in keeping with that old line about the Romans: When in church do those things which are related to the church, and when at home, concentrate on family activities.

Such a false dichotomy was unknown in the days of the New Testament. As a matter of fact, there were no church buildings until almost the third century and local congregations most often met in homes for their fellowship gatherings. In fact, fellowship is one of the New Testament patterns which relates to both church and home. Charles M. Sell writes:

The church is the fellowship of families united to inform, strengthen, and inspire one another. The family is a fellowship of parents, relatives and children whose day by day inter-relationships provide the most dynamic possibilities for warmth and love. This is why the pluralistic expression of Christian fellowship in the Word of God (Colossians, chapter 3) is blended into Paul's instructions on both church and home.

One of the problems we face in this relationship in the 20th century is a hesitancy on the part of church leaders to tackle the really difficult problems of family life. Most pastors, for example, are quite happy to stay away from subects like premarital sex, early marriages and divorce. One pastor of a reasonably large church told me just a short time ago that he never mentions his views on divorce publicly. If people want to hear what he has to say, he will talk about it in the privacy of his study.

At first glance that sounds like a most discreet way of handling a touchy subject. A thorough view of the situation, however, should uncover the simple fact that if divorce and the relationship of partners in marriage is really a Biblical standard, then even if views differ among evangelicals the issue is a part of "the whole counsel of God" and must be dealt with in a preaching ministry. Statistics tell us various things about divorce in our country and one can use them to substantiate almost any case. One thing is clear, however; divorce rates are on the rapid increase and there is no reason to believe that the increase will not continue during this decade. What is even more frightening is that many Christian couples who would never go openly to a court of law live in a state of "practical divorce" pretending to play the game but not enjoying the warm relationships which must be a strategic part of any Christian marriage.

Let's not minimize the difficulty of the church's task. It has to build and strengthen Christian homes within the evil context of a disintegrating society. The cynical rhetorical question which the hymn writer asked has never been more relevant than in the sensuous 70s: "Is this vile world a friend to grace to help me on to God?" The almost invisible standards of the hippie culture; the warped ethics which teach children and young people to expect something for nothing; the urbanization and industrialization which tears people from the land and throws them into a whirlpool of constant mobility; the equalization of the sexes screamed at television cameras by bra-less females searching for a role which they have already abandoned; and the hopeless secularization of the entire social milieu combine to make up a formidable foe. One tends to recall the words of Moses recorded in the 28th Chapter of the book of Deuteronomy, "You will watch as your sons and daughters are taken away as slaves. Your heart will break with longing for them, but you will not be able to help them" (Deuteronomy 28:32, *The Living Bible*).

Progress in Church-Home Relations

There seems to be (at least in the field of Christian Education) a renewed interest in church-home relations. Some local churches are beginning to realize that the teaching and preaching ministries which they carry on are exercised largely in the theoretical realm. They are beginning to admit that the home must be the laboratory for practical application of these Biblical ideals. Another good sign is the interest on the part of many churches in a total Christian education program. Rather than just Sunday school and evangelistic services held together by a string of buses, churches are beginning to deliberately construct programs for families. They are making an effort to teach the family what the church is all about and to listen to the needs and interests of the family itself. Loyalty becomes not only something the family owes to its church, but also a commitment the church has to its families. Home Bible classes and family camping are among the most dynamic and growing educational agencies being carried on in many local churches today. Both are family-centered ministries.

We've also seen a significant number of books and articles appearing which center attention on the Christian home. Family Life Education Conferences are taking their place alongside Missionary Conferences, Bible Conferences, and Prophecy Conferences as regular annual functions in many local churches. Pastors are beginning to preach more on the subject of the family and Sunday school curricula are including units on the Christian home. Without doubt interest in the Christian home is one of the most healthy and significant trends in the Christian education movements in our day.

Proposals for Improving Church-Home Relations

There is still much land to be conquered. For one thing, the church must get serious about premarital counseling. Actually, we ought to be talking about pre-marital **education** and not just counseling. The latter refers to that short period of time (a few weeks at the maximum and a few minutes at the minimum) during which the pastor tends to establish some foundational principles for the development of a new Christian home. By that time, attitudes have been largely solidified and we can't expect much change. Family life education should be going on constantly in both church and home.

Another step in the right direction would be for the church to get serious about adult education. They are draft dodgers in the battle to stamp out Biblical illiteracy. Howard Hendricks tells the story of a highly educated man in an evangelical church who had just witnessed his first ordination council. After watching the young ministerial candidate being questioned by the council for several hours, the man concluded that he had heard more Biblical truth in that one day than he had learned in the church in 20 years. He rushed up to

Dr. Hendricks, laid hands on him bodily and said, "Why don't you teach us like that?"

Still another front for attack on family disintegration is the emphasis on family evangelism. Too long we have gone after children or young people without selling the idea that Christ is for the whole family and He wants entire families. Sometimes it isn't possible to win an entire family to the Savior and then we should rejoice at whatever fruit God enables us to have. But it is our **emphasis** on the issue which is crucial. What are we trying to do? What kind of family-centered evangelistic programming are we developing in evangelical churches? In the Scripture Press Christian Education Monograph series, Dr. Roy Zuck urges pastors to "make Christianity family business" and says:

> If a pastor is interested in reaching children and young people for the Lord and helping them grow in Him, he will be interested in ministering to families. One pastor remarked, "Everything else we do finally succeeds or fails under God, depending on the home."

Finally the church can avoid conflict with the home by establishing a program which does not monopolize evening time. Some church bulletins read as though they were deliberately calculated to divide the family by making sure one member had to be present at the church every evening of the week. A pastor told me not too long ago that he **deliberately** schedules church activities this way because, "They don't know what to do with themselves at home anyway. They just sit around and watch television." What he apparently failed to realize is that he has the strategic responsibility to teach families what to do at home. Where do young parents learn how to relate to each other, to their children, and to God if they cannot learn it in the church? Many churches have become so concerned about over-programming that they now conduct what has been called a mid-week "Family Night." Prayer meeting, club programs, and whatever else will fit are scheduled that evening. With the exception of the family night, Sunday evening, and perhaps one other night given to visitation or choir rehearsal, the family is free to spend time at home or in other activities together.

We've come a long way from "the Cotter's Saturday night" and it is quite clear that we cannot return to that simple and spiritual kind of family life. Nevertheless, God's priorities have not been realigned and the Scripture has not been rewritten. The single most important agency for Christian nurture is the home and the church is only properly carrying out its task when it focuses its ministries on families and enables rather than hinders the teaching activities of parents.

Oh, my people, listen to my teaching. Open your ears to what I am saying for I will show you lessons from our history, stories handed down to us from former generations. I will reveal these truths to you so that you can describe these glorious deeds of Jehovah to your children, and tell them about the mighty miracles he did. For he gave his laws to Israel, and commanded our fathers to teach them to our children, so that they in turn could teach their children too. Thus his law passed down from generation to generation. In this way each generation has been able to obey his laws and to set its hope anew on God and not forget his glorious miracles (Psalm 78:1-7 *The Living Bible*).

Epilogue

Letter To Jeff

Dear Son,

Last night I came home late, sometime after midnight. As I have done many times before, I walked slowly into your room to kiss you good night, even though you had been asleep for several hours. At moments like this I look at you and think about the eleven years that we've shared together. They have been good years and I think back on them with warmth and happiness. There's a love between us, son, that is built on a mutual respect which calls forth obedience and kindness into a happy bond of camaraderie. Oh, I know you really don't know what that word means, but it really doesn't make any difference because I'm not talking about things now that you can understand. Perhaps they are even things that I do not understand.

You see, I'm looking beyond this day. A few years beyond. To the time when you will be a "teen-ager"— those so-called critical and turbulent years which misunderstanding adults have mistakenly made into a narrow valley of traumatic experiences through which a child must pass before he can become a man.

You know what some are saying, son? Psychologists, educators, clergymen, all alike. They are telling us that we won't be able to speak to each other, or at least not understand each other, in just a few more years.

134

Oh, you'll probably reside here in the house, and we'll have meals together and see each other occasionally, but we're supposed to live in two different worlds. They call it a "generation gap."

A generation gap?—well—it's just rather hard to explain, Jeff. I suppose like a lot of things we talk about now it connotes different ideas to different people. What it means is that the values, morals and ideas that I hold, believe in, and live by just aren't relevant for your day and that you'll have to go out and find some of your own. You are supposed to challenge all the things that dad stands for. Show some healthy signs of rebellion to prove to your friends (and to the sociologists) that you're not apathetic about the world in which you live.

Oh, this generation gap covers just about everything in our lives, son. It deals with small things like music and clothes, and goes all the way to feelings of obedience to your parents, loyalty to your country, and faith in God. It's just not good to conform. Of course, since **all** teen-agers are expected to be nonconformists, I guess you'll just have to end up conforming to nonconformity.

It's really all based on philosophical relativism. That means that people think nothing is sure from year to year or even from day to day. They think that everything has to be questioned and expect that the questioning will probably result in change. This whole philosophy basically assumes that things are bad just because they're old and, I suppose, consequently that things are good just because they're new. It's the disease of presentism.

But you haven't been taught this way, son. You've been taught that there are absolutes, things which are fixed for all eternity by the determination of God. You have learned that there are certain standards which are set, not by society, but which come from a code far beyond the shifting views of man. You've been taught that love, obedience, faith, and honesty are virtues in any age and in any situation. If you believe what you've been taught, and try to live this way, you will be subjected to criticism and scoffing by the society in which you live. May God give you the courage to face it!

Well, maybe now you can begin to see why I wonder what lies ahead for us, young friend. Five years from now, will we still take bike rides together and talk about things that we're both interested in? Will we still sit on the living room floor and listen to Beethoven on one record and the Kingston Trio on the next and enjoy them both together? Will we go to church together and believe that what the Pastor says is true because he's preaching about truths that are timeless? Oh, I know you'll think dad is square because he won't wear some of the clothes that happen to be in fashion for young men. You might not even like some of the rules that we will still have to maintain as long as you're living at our house. But will these little differences actually drive a wedge between us that can be called a "generation gap?"

I know if you were awake right now you would put your arms around my neck and tell me, "No, dad. Nothing can come between us like that. We'll always be together just as we are now." And I'd like to hear you say it, and I'd like to believe it. But we will really have to wait those several years to find out the answer to my questions here by your bedside tonight. Good night, son. I hope the future allows us to build a bridge across the gap.

BIBLIOGRAPHY

Adams, Theodore F. *Making Your Marriage Succeed*. New York: Harper Bros., 1953.

Amstutz, H. Clair, M.D. *Growing Up To Love: A Guide To Sex Education For Parents*. Scottdale, Pa.: Herald Press, 1956.

Anderson, Doris. *How to Raise a Christian Family*. Grand Rapids: Zondervan, 1960.

Bell, Donald A. *The Family in Dialogue*. Grand Rapids: Zondervan, 1968.

Bowman, Henry A. *A Christian Interpretation of Marriage*. Philadelphia: The Westminster Press, 1959.

Brandt, Henry R. and Homer E. Dowdy. *Building A Christian Home*. Wheaton, Ill.: Scripture Press, second prntg. 1961.

Butterfield, Oliver M. *Sexual Harmony in Marriage*. New York: Emerson Books, Inc. n.d.

Bye, Beryl. *Teaching Our Children the Christian Faith*. Chicago: Moody Press, 1966.

Capper, W. Melville and Morgan H. Williams. *Toward Christian Marriage*. Chicago: Inter-Varsity Press, 1958.

Carrington, William L., M.D. *The Healing of Marriage*. Great Neck, L. I., New York: Channel Press, 1961.

Channels, Vera. *The Layman Builds A Christian Home*. St. Louis: Bethany, 1959.

Christenson, Larry. *The Christian Family*. Minneapolis: Bethany Fellowship, 1970.

Cole, Wm. Graham. *Sex and Love in the Bible*. New York: Association Press, 1959.

The Concordia Sex Education Series. W. J. Fields (ed.) St. Louis, Mo.: Concordia Publishing House, 1967

Crouch, W. Perry. *Guidance for Christian Home Life*. Nashville: Convention Press, 1955.

Deen, Edith. *Family Living in the Bible*. New York: Harper and Row, 1963.

DeJong, Alexander. *The Christian Family and Home*. Grand Rapids: Baker Book House, 1959.

Dobson, James. *Dare to Discipline*. Wheaton, Illinois: Tyndale House, 1970.

Duvall, Evelyn M., and Reuben Hill. *Being Married*. Boston: D. C. Heath and Company 1960.

DuVall, Evelyn M. *Why Wait Till Marriage?*, New York: Association Press, 1965.

Eavey, Charles B. *Principles of Personality Building for Christian Parents*. Grand Rapids: Zondervan Publishing House, 1952.

Engagement and Marriage. Marriage and Family Research Series. St. Louis, Mo.: Concordia Publishing House, 1959.

Erb. Alta Mae. *Christian Education in the Home*. Scottdale, Pa.: Herald Press, 1963.

——————. *Christian Nurture of Children*. Scottdale, Pa.: Herald Press, rev. 1955.

Fairchild, Roy and John C. Wynn. *Families in the Church*. New York: Association Press, 1961.

Fallaw, Wesner B. *The Modern Parent and the Teaching Church*. New York: Macmillan, 1946.

Feucht, Oscar E. (ed.) *Helping Families Through the Church*. St. Louis: Concordia Publishing House, 1957.

——————, et al., *The Family That Makes It*. Wheaton, Illinois, Scripture Press, 1971.

Fisher-Hunter, W. *The Divorce Problem*. Waynesboro, Pa.: Macneish Publishers, 1952.

Getz, Gene A. *The Christian Home*. Chicago, Ill.: Moody Bible Institute, 1967.

Hart, W. Neill. *Home and Church Working Together*. Nashville: Abingdon, 1951.

Jacobsen, Margaret Bailey. *The Child in the Christian Home*: *A Practical Psychology for Christian Parents and Church Workers*. Wheaton, Ill.: Scripture Press, 1959.

Lewin and Gilmore. *Sex Without Fear*. New York: Medical Research Press, 1950.

Matthews, Charles A. *The Christian Home*. Cincinnati: Standard, n.d.

Miles, Herbert J. *Sexual Happiness in Marriage*. Grand Rapids: Zondervan, 1967.

Miller, Basil. *The Minister's Marriage Manual*. Dallas: Chandler Publications, 1955.

Narramore, Clyde M. *How to Succeed in Family Living*. Glendale, Cal.: G/L Publications, 1968.

——————. *How to Tell Your Children About Sex*. Grand Rapids: Zondervan Publishing House, 1958.

——————. *How to Understand and Influence Young People*. Grand Rapids, Mich.: Zondervan Publishing House, 1957.

_____. *Life and Love — A Christian View of Sex*. Grand Rapids, Mich.: Zondervan Publishing House, 1956.

_____. *Psychology of Counseling*. Grand Rapids: Zondervan Publishing Co., 1960.

Overton, Grace S. *Living with Parents*. Nashville: Broadman Press, 1954.

Rehwinkle, Alfred Martin. *Planned Parenthood*. St. Louis: Concordia Publishing House, 1959.

Scudder, C. W. *The Family in Christian Perspective*. Nashville, Tenn.: Broadman Press, 1962.

Small, Dwight Hervey. *Design for Christian Marriage*. Westwood, N. J.: Fleming H. Revell, 1959.

_____. *After You've Said I Do*. Westwood, N. J.: Fleming H. Revell, 1968.

Stewart, Charles William. *The Minister As Marriage Counselor*. Nashville, Tenn.: Abingdon Press, 1961.

Trobisch, Walter. *I Loved A Girl*. New York: Harper and Row, 1968.

_____. *I Married You*. New York: Harper and Row, 1971.

_____. *Love Is A Feeling To Be Learned*. Downers Grove, Ill.: Inter-Varsity Press, 1968.

_____. *My Parents Are Impossible*. Downers Grove, Ill.: Inter-Varsity Press, 1971.

_____. *My Wife Made Me A Polygamist*. Downers Grove, Ill.: Inter-Varsity Press, 1971.

_____. *Please Help Me, Please Love Me*. Downers Grove, Ill.: Inter-Varsity Press, 1970.

Trueblood, Elton, and Pauline Trueblood. *The Recovery of Family Life*. New York: Harper & Brothers, 1953.

Vaughn, Ruth. *What I Will Tell My Children About God*. Kansas City, Mo.: Beacon Hill Press, second prntg. 1966.

Wilkerson, David R. *Parents on Trial*. New York: Hawthorn Books, 1967.

Wynn, John Charles. *How Christian Parents Face Family Problems*. Philadelphia: The Westminster Press, 1955.

Wyrtzen, Jack. *Sex and the Bible*. Grand Rapids: Zondervan Publishing Co., 1958.

Zuck, Roy B. and Gene A. Getz, editors. *Adult Education in the Church*. Chicago: Moody Press, 1970.

Zuck, Roy B. and Gene A. Getz, editors. *Ventures in Family Living*. Chicago: Moody Press, 1970.